THE WORST GIG

FROM PSYCHO FANS TO STAGE RIOTS, FAMOUS MUSICIANS TELL ALL

JON NICCUM

Published by Sourcebooks, Inc.
P.O. Box 4410, Naperville, Illinois 60567–4410
(630) 961–3900
Fax: (630) 961–2168
www.sourcebooks.com

Library of Congress Cataloging-in-Publication Data

Niccum, Jon.
  The worst gig : from psycho fans to stage riots, famous musicians tell all / Jon Niccum.
    pages cm
  (trade paper : alk. paper) 1. Musicians—Anecdotes. 2. Musicians—Interviews. I. Title.
  ML65.N33 2013
  781.64–dc23

                        2013023162

        Printed and bound in the United States of America
            VP 10 9 8 7 6 5 4 3 2 1

FOR ALL THE MUSIC MAKERS

CONTENTS

INTRODUCTION VI

CHAPTER ONE:
WRONG VENUE 1

COWBOY JUNKIES 2
ALICE COOPER 6
OWL CITY 8
FISHBONE 10
KANSAS 13
PAT METHENY 14
CROSS CANADIAN RAGWEED 16
GRACE POTTER AND THE NOCTURNALS 18
GILLIAN WELCH 23
GWAR 24
THE GET UP KIDS 27
"Tales of Touring Terror: The Screamin'
Sirens' Worst Gig," by Pleasant Gehman 28

CHAPTER TWO:
INSANE FANS 35

RUSH 36
MUTEMATH 38
JULIANA HATFIELD 41
AFTER THE FIRE 42
INXS 45
MIKE WATT 46
RUFUS WAINWRIGHT 49
TENACIOUS D 50
BETTIE SERVEERT 51
X 52

"Poster Children's Colorful Array of
Crappy Gigs," by Rose Marshack 55

CHAPTER THREE:
DANGEROUS
MALFUNCTIONS 61

FLAMING LIPS 62
DWEEZIL ZAPPA 66
UME 68
RENAISSANCE 71
YUNG SKEETER 72
OTEP 75
BELLE AND SEBASTIAN 76
WILCO 79
"The French-ish Connection,"
by Jason Falkner 80

CHAPTER FOUR:
COMMUNICATION
BREAKDOWN 83

FLOGGING MOLLY 84
DROWNING POOL 89
JOHN SCOFIELD 90
BERNARD PURDIE 92
TREASURE FINGERS 94
MOBY GRAPE 97
NEW DUNCAN IMPERIALS 98
BILL LYNCH 100
KINKY FRIEDMAN 102
R/D 104

STEVE LUKATHER 108

"Semisonic's Worst Shows Ever: A
Conference Call," by Dan Wilson 113

CHAPTER FIVE: MOTHER NATURE'S WRATH 125

GARBAGE 126

CONCRETE BLONDE 130

DEF LEPPARD 132

FITZ AND THE TANTRUMS 134

GEORGE WINSTON 137

TOWER OF POWER 138

"Eisley Braves the Snowpocalypse,"
by Sherri DuPree-Bemis 141

CHAPTER SIX: OOPS! 147

JANE'S ADDICTION 148

BLUE MAN GROUP 150

LAURIE ANDERSON 152

JOHN MAYER 154

12TH PLANET 156

CHAMBERLIN 158

NADA SURF 161

PETER FRAMPTON 162

RUBBLEBUCKET 164

BORGORE 166

DAUGHTRY 168

ANTHRAX 170

"BR549's Stomach-Turning Worst
Show," by Chuck Mead 172

CHAPTER SEVEN: VIOLENCE 177

THE SEX PISTOLS 178

JOE SATRIANI 182

TOOL 185

MIKE FINNIGAN 186

HENRY ROLLINS 189

TRANSLATOR 190

LOS LONELY BOYS 192

JEFFERSON STARSHIP 194

"Fugazi under Siege in Warsaw!"
by Ian MacKaye 196

CHAPTER EIGHT: IT'S ALL GOOD 203

TORI AMOS 204

INCUBUS 206

THE WALLFLOWERS 207

THAT 1 GUY 208

AIMEE MANN 211

THE PRESIDENTS OF THE UNITED STATES
OF AMERICA 212

CHELY WRIGHT 214

WYNTON MARSALIS 216

THE LOST BROTHERS 218

DRIVIN' 'N' CRYIN' 220

LED ZEPPELIN 223

"Indescribably Not of This Earth,"
by Ted Nugent 224

AFTERWORD: THE AUTHOR'S OWN WORST GIG

"Bloody Wichita," by Jon Niccum 227

ACKNOWLEDGMENTS 230

ABOUT THE AUTHOR 231

INTRODUCTION

I began interviewing "famous musicians" as a print journalist in 1994, primarily doing advance "phoners" for acts that were touring through the Kansas City market. Typically, I'd spend several hours doing research and then map out a dozen or more questions in advance that were specifically tailored to an artist.

One time an overseas call from the guitarist for The Cranberries arrived six hours earlier than scheduled, catching me off guard and underprepared. Following that, I assembled a batch of my favorite questions in a document called "Generic Interview," in case something similar happened again. These questions were ones that usually inspired worthy replies:

+ "What's the best advice you've received about playing music?"
+ "Do you have any superstitions or rituals that you follow to prepare for a show?"
+ "What line from one of your songs do people ask you the most about?"
+ "What's been your career highlight?"

The last question appeared reasonably provocative, but I noticed it never generated an answer worth publishing. The responses were either too gushy or prosaic. So I decided to try the opposite tactic during a few interviews, asking, "What is the worst show you've ever played?"

That question unleashed the most brutally colorful stories.

Since then, most of the performers I've interviewed have revealed their "worst gig." When many of these salty chronicles proved unprintable in a daily newspaper, I proceeded to hoard them. I knew that someday they would find a proper home elsewhere.

In 2011, I launched the website The Worst Gig (worstgig.com), and the reaction was immediate. The site was written up all over the place, from BuzzFeed to Gorilla Mask, and the accompanying web traffic was outstanding. After Salon raved about the site with the headline "Musicians' 'Worst Gig' makes for best read ever," I knew the stories wouldn't remain limited to the Internet.

Now after hundreds of interviews with national headliners, the project has made it into actual print, which is right where it started.

The Worst Gig features unique tales told directly to me by the artists. Most of these I gathered through phone interviews or in-person conversations, with a few longer accounts penned specifically for the book. The collection delves into the times when things didn't quite work out for performers—be it because of equipment breakdowns, psychotic fans, awkward mix-ups, violent confrontations or nature's wrath. These incidents may have seemed horrifying, mortifying or unendurable at the time, but in the rearview mirror, they prove hilarious. Sometimes the worst shows inspire the best stories.

—JON NICCUM

Chapter
-1-
WRONG VENUE

WHAT HAPPENS WHEN HARD ROCK BANDS GET BOOKED AT RELIGIOUS VENUES, POP ARTISTS TAKE THE STAGE AT METAL FESTIVALS AND MUSICIANS FIND THEMSELVES PLAYING ODDBALL PLACES THAT SHOULD NEVER, EVER FEATURE BANDS.

COWBOY JUNKIES

The antithesis of the loud, distorted music of the alternative-rock boom, Toronto's Cowboy Junkies became known for quieter, haunting material that explored country, blues and folk. Sustaining the same sibling-loaded lineup since 1985, the band features singer Margo Timmins, guitarist Michael Timmins, drummer Peter Timmins and bassist Alan Anton. (Margo Timmins once netted the People *magazine distinction of being one of "the 50 most beautiful people in the world.") The quartet's indelible venture remains* The Trinity Sessions, *an acclaimed 1987 album recorded with a single ambisonic microphone at Toronto's Church of the Holy Trinity. In 2007, the band released* Trinity Revisited, *a reinterpretation of the previous album featuring guest appearances by Ryan Adams, Natalie Merchant and Vic Chesnutt.*

◆ ◆ ◆

"The worst, worst, worst one that sort of affected me for life was our first major record-label gig. This would have been '89, so we were not a young band, but we were new to the corporate world. We'd signed to RCA, and they were having their international conference. So all the heads from around the world were meeting in Marbella, Spain, to drink and get stupid. We were sort of going to be the surprise new act that they'd signed. A lot of them didn't know we were signed to RCA. That's what they do: They all stand up and say who they signed and what their plans are. Blah, blah, blah.

"So they had this big dinner up on top of a mountain

where there was this famous bullring—like a private bullring—and it had a dining area. The only way to get to it was to get on the bus from the hotel and go there. So all these corporate dudes were pretty much trapped up there for all sorts of conference things: lots of speeches, lots of drinking, lots of eating. It goes on and on. We're stuffed in the bullring area, which was OK—we didn't want to be in the party—and we're waiting to be told to go on and play.

"It's now really late, and they are pissed drunk and tired. Just as we are about to go out, Heinz Henn, who was the president of the company in the States, comes up to me and says in his German accent—which I can't do, but it was very stern—'I want you to sing "Mining for Gold."'" And I never sang [a cappella] 'Mining for Gold' in those days. It was not that I was shy, but I was not confident.

"I was like, 'I can't do that.'

"He was like, 'No, you have to sing it. You have to sing it.'

"Again, in those days you're feeling as a band that every gig is so important, and you've got to do what you got to do. I don't know what I thought. I wish it was now and I could have turned to him and said, 'Go away!'

"And the boys were like, 'Look, Margo, we'll stand up behind you and get up onstage so you're not alone.'

"So I go out, and the place is either everybody's talking or they're literally asleep. There's a guy sitting in front of me—and I'll never forget his face. He's a Japanese guy, and he's, like, drunk-asleep. His head is back in the most uncomfortable way, his mouth is wide open, and he's drooling. And he's snoring.

"I'm like, 'This is hell.'

"They don't care. It's late. I'm tired. They're tired. Everybody wants to go home, and they're trapped. They can't go until we've done our thing.

"Heinz comes out and introduces us like they just signed U2 or something. So we go out, and I start to sing 'Mining for Gold.' The guy is snoring, like loud. I'm beginning to lose it because I can't focus. I can't find anybody to focus on. Nobody's listening. And then I look up and there's one guy listening, and he has a very large head. He's staring, like, piercingly staring, from across the room.

"I'm like, 'OK, I'm going to focus on that guy.'

"As I'm focusing on him I go, 'I know that guy. It's Gene Simmons of Kiss!'

"I'm like, 'I can't do this. I'm in some sort of weird alter-world. I don't know what's happening to me.'

"So we do our gig. No one listens except for Gene. Through the whole deal I was bonding with him. 'Thank you for listening.'

"He came up afterward, and he totally knew the gig.

"He said, 'That was a hard gig.'

"And I said, 'Just tell me they get better.'"

—MARGO TIMMINS, COWBOY JUNKIES

ALICE COOPER

There would be no Kiss without him. No Rob Zombie. No Slipknot. And certainly no Marilyn Manson. Alice Cooper was, and continues to be, the undisputed father of shock rock, a title he's embraced since the late 1960s. The Detroit native and member since 2011 of the Rock and Roll Hall of Fame is best known for his classic rock hits "School's Out," "I'm Eighteen" and "No More Mr. Nice Guy." And who could forget Cooper's immortal appearance playing himself in the film Wayne's World?

I don't think that we've ever done a bad show. I can say that honestly. I always design our shows so that there's no such thing as a bad show. The audience won't know if we play a bad show. We will, but they won't. But you get audiences sometimes that are just asleep. I don't care what you do, they just will not wake up.

"The worst one was at [University of Guelph], in [Ontario] Canada, back in the '70s, where by the end of the fifth song we turned around and played to the walls. Then we found out that The Kinks were there the week before, and after about the fourth or fifth song they turned around and played to the walls. They did the exact thing we did, the audience was so dead…It's an agricultural college. The people were sitting in Samsonite chairs holding hands.

"'Now here's Alice Cooper…'

"They just sat there and would not move. I didn't know if they were threatened, like, 'If you move you're going to get expelled or something.'

"Out of the thousands of shows we've played, that was the one show I can remember as being the worst show."

—ALICE COOPER

OWL CITY

CREDIT: MATT VOGEL

Adam Young is the brainchild behind Owl City, a poppy electronica project that the Minnesota-raised artist created to thwart his bouts with insomnia. Young attained massive buzz through online grassroots networking and released two indie albums before finally inking with Universal Republic. Owl City's ensuing major-label debut, **Ocean Eyes,** *featured the number-one hit "Fireflies," which went quadruple Platinum. He followed that up in 2012 with the top-ten hit "Good Time," a duet with Carly Rae Jepsen.*

♦ ♦ ♦

"The worst show I ever played was at a local county fair in rural Iowa. They had the bands playing in a smelly old hog barn with *actual* hogs rooting around. Nobody showed up, so it was just us and the porkers. It was intense. Actually, now that I think of it, it might've been the *best* show I've ever played."

—ADAM YOUNG, OWL CITY

FISHBONE

Assembled in the late 1970s at a Los Angeles middle school when mandatory busing brought inner-city kids to predominately white schools in the San Fernando Valley, Fishbone scored a record deal with Columbia before all the members were out of high school. The ensemble dispensed some of the most accomplished music of the pre-grunge era, mixing ska, metal, rap, funk, reggae, punk and soul into a boisterous jumble as entertaining as it was ambitious. Still together decades later—powered by two of the founding members, Angelo Moore (vocals and saxophone) and Norwood Fisher (bass)—the group recently made front-page headlines when the house band on Late Night with Jimmy Fallon *played its song "Lyin' Ass Bitch" to accompany the appearance of former Republican presidential candidate Michele Bachmann.*

◆ ◆ ◆

"There was a gig in our career before we were Fishbone, but we were the same six members. This is the gig that got us to change our name to Fishbone because we were called Megatron—which we can all agree was a bad name. We had just gotten new management and he booked us at this club called the Music Machine in West LA. He put us on this bill that was all heavy-metal bands. The booker at the club thought—based on our name—that this would fit. Maybe he thought we were Megadeth? We were doing what we do, and we did not fit with any of the bands. It was a horrible show. There were probably like eight people in the audience, and my grandmother was one of them…[Another bad show] was with the original six guys early in our career. We had changed our name to Fishbone, and our manager got us a show to open a Trak Auto Parts store in Compton [California], playing the parking lot of a shopping center. No one booed us. No one threw anything at us. But we got the strangest looks. It was the wrong band in the wrong part of town doing the wrong music. For once we actually bothered people more than we brought joy into their hearts."

—NORWOOD FISHER, FISHBONE

KANSAS

Debuting as White Clover in 1970, the ensemble from Topeka, Kansas, kicked around for a few years before solidifying a lineup and changing its name to one that matched the members' license plates. Eventually, music mogul Don Kirshner became interested in the group's not-very-radio-friendly mix of progressive rock and rural emotion. Decades of basically the same lineup and sales of thirty million records followed. The band's hits "Carry On Wayward Son," "Dust in the Wind" and "Point of Know Return" continue to be staples of classic-rock airplay.

"One of the most memorable ones we played was up in Wisconsin, called Nudestock. It was a nudist colony. Foreigner was on the bill and Alan Parsons. But you expect up in Wisconsin there'd be all these beautiful blond women. But the reality is never what you imagine. You get there and it looks like you walked into a Piggly Wiggly grocery store and suddenly everybody was naked. And you're standing there playing and there's some guy with a baseball hat and tennis shoes standing in front of you, wiggling and playing air guitar with his pecker swirling around. It bothers you."

—RICH WILLIAMS, KANSAS

PAT METHENY

Jazz is often divided into the traditionalists and the risk takers. Pat Metheny considers himself a proud member of the latter set. For five decades the Missouri native has been releasing acclaimed albums, each one a new wrinkle in the development of jazz. Although best known for his freelance ventures and work with The Pat Metheny Group, the guitarist has enjoyed numerous collaborations, ranging from such stylistic stalwarts as Dave Brubeck to fellow experimentalists Herbie Hancock and Ornette Coleman to pop-music idols David Bowie and Joni Mitchell. And he's dabbled in the world of film and television, composing soundtracks for features including **The Falcon and the Snowman** and **A Map of the World**. Along the way he's racked up an astonishing nineteen Grammy Awards.

"I once was hired to play on a jazz festival in Palermo, Italy. The trio that I had at that time was [with] Charlie Hayden and Billy Higgins. First of all, we got to the gig and there were signs everywhere that said Pat Metheny Group. And what we were playing was nothing like that. I was completely freaked out about that. Then they said, 'We'll take you to the venue.'

"So we started driving through Palermo, and I noticed that we were getting closer and closer to what appeared to be the largest soccer stadium on the island of Sicily.

"I was like, 'No!'

"Sure enough, that's where we were playing. We get there, and I notice that the stage is in the direct center of the soccer field. It's 150 yards from the stands. I'm thinking they're going to let people come out on the grass and they'll all be standing around the thing. We get out there, and there were barriers around the stage.

"I'm like, 'Can we move these barriers and let people get closer?'

"The guy looked at me and said, 'We don't let anybody on the grass.'

"So the nearest person is like half a football field away in this stadium that seated about seventy thousand people—and there were about twenty thousand people there. And the PA they had was basically like the kind you'd have at a wedding. Plus, Charlie and Billy were the softest rhythm section in jazz. So we did our best, but that was a pretty rough night. It was just surreal and wrong."

—*PAT METHENY*

CROSS CANADIAN RAGWEED

The group Cross Canadian Ragweed was cooked up by singer Cody Canada, guitarist Grady Cross, drummer Randy Ragsdale and bassist Jeremy Plato—its name derived from a combination of Cross, Canada and Ragsdale. The band honed its sound in the early 1990s while based in Stillwater, Oklahoma. In 2001, the members relocated to Texas, developing a rabid following—in part because of extensive touring—before disbanding nine years later. The quartet became emblematic of the American Red Dirt movement known for merging country and rock.

"It was Gordon, Nebraska. It was the biggest shithole gig we've played. We'd been on a seven-week run…Everybody was missing home and missing families. We'd actually come home for one day for a friend of ours' birthday party. Then we turned around and went to Gordon, Nebraska. We'd just been there. It was under one hundred miles from Sturgis [South Dakota], and we'd just played Sturgis. We thought, 'This better be a pretty kick-ass gig if we're taking two days off just to drive.'

"We got there and it was in an outside rodeo arena. The trailer we played on had particleboard sides and roof, and they had gotten it stuck in all the cow shit and horse shit earlier that day. They were trying to pull the stage out and they swung shit all over—so it was green, dried crap. They asked us to have a bite to eat because they were cooking steaks. We were sitting in the horse-stall area, and there were flies buzzing all over the food. People were actually sitting in piles of horse shit.

"The guy walked up to our road manager and said, 'You know, Randy Travis said this is the worst gig he ever played.'

"We thought, 'Why in the hell would you repeat that?'

"They were harping on us all day to play country-friendly songs for the crowd because there were a lot of older people there who were sponsors. But we said, 'You hired us, so we're going to play what we are.'

"Halfway through the set, the guy came up to our road manager and asked if we could finish the night playing nothing but Willie Nelson—which if it was our idea, we'd have done it.

"That was the worst gig ever. Usually our contract is ninety minutes, and we play two hours and fifteen minutes. But that was one of those where right when the clock hits that ninety-minute mark, 'We're out of here!'"

–CODY CANADA, CROSS CANADIAN RAGWEED

GRACE POTTER AND THE NOCTURNALS

Grace Potter possesses one of the most commanding voices of any singer on the festival circuit. The multi-instrumentalist developed the group Grace Potter and the Nocturnals in 2002 while attending St. Lawrence University. Soon her Vermont-based act was logging two hundred shows a year before it had even released a proper record. The band's style has been described as "a modern-day version of Tina Turner stroking the microphone in a spangled mini-dress while fronting The Rolling Stones circa 'Sticky Fingers.'" Elsewhere, the Nocturnals can be heard performing Jefferson Airplane's "White Rabbit" on the companion soundtrack for Tim Burton's Alice in Wonderland. Potter also wrote and performed "Something That I Want," the credits track on Disney's animated hit Tangled.

◆ ◆ ◆

We've been touring for I would say, realistically—nationally—about six or seven years. And when we were just getting started, I have not just a worst gig but a worst tour. It's all connected.

"We were asked to go on tour with a huge star. Our booking agent was like, 'Well, what you're going to be doing is playing [as] the second-stage band. This particular star wants to have a very *festivally* vibe wherever he tours. So you'll be the band that's by the beer tent the whole time.'

"We were like, 'Oh, that's so great. We're on tour with so-and-so. This is going to be killer.'

"I think it was three months over the course

of a summer. We just sort of picked up in major cities—we're going from arena to arena. We'd look at our schedule, and it was like, 'Oh my God, it's the Verizon Wireless Amphitheatre here, and the Nissan Center there, and the casino over here. This is gonna be great.'

"So we get there on the first day, and not only are we not in the beer-tent area, we're actually in the parking lot. And the stage had no mic booms. It was meant to be [that] we were gonna bring our own sound, I guess. Nothing was really advanced. So every single place we went we thought, 'OK, so cool. We'll have our backstage passes, so at least we'll be able to go backstage.'

"Well, we found out the first day that not only were we not allowed backstage, we weren't allowed to park where the normal fans were allowed to park. We had to park off-site and walk our stuff on. So we were allowed to come in, pull up, unload our gear, but then park our car off-site because we 'didn't want to get in the way of the fans.' So we'd have this mile walk between wherever the stage was, and we were supposed to bring our own sound.

"We fixed that problem, luckily, and by the end of the first day, at least there were mic booms onstage.

"And then there was the infamous Red Rocks. Three nights at Red Rocks [in Colorado], which was unbelievable. Finally, we got the invitation to go backstage after touring with this guy for several months…We were starving and poor, and they said, 'Sure, come get some catering or whatever.'

"So I got catering not just for me but for the whole band because not everybody was allowed backstage; it was just me. So I come out of the catering area with every piece of food I could get. After three months of touring I felt like I earned this food, right? So I'm walking with all this food in my hands. I've got plate after plate after plate of lamb and all this good stuff. 'Wow, we haven't eaten this well in a long time.'

"I feed the band. Everybody's happy. It's the end of the night. The third night at Red Rocks. Of course, we weren't *at* Red Rocks on the main stage. We were up in a little baby tent somewhere. Then we continued on our tour. About a week later I got a phone call from my booking agent saying, 'Yeah, about that catering you took. I just got a $350 bill…'

"It was just one thing after another. And every once in a while I tried to zip backstage and grab a shower. Sometimes I would sneak in. But one time the big star was walking down the hallway. So all this security locked down the hallway. They're like, 'We've got a bogey!' And I was the bogey…because I was in the shower.

"So there's a security guard standing in front of the door not letting me out. I'm in a towel trying to get back out to my bus…I'm dripping wet. I don't have my hair dryer or anything with me because they said I could only be in there for like five minutes. So I'm hiding behind a door and there's a security guard literally telling me that I can't go anywhere.

"I said, 'Can I at least get out of the bathroom and get my clothing, which is in that other room?'

"I go into the other room, and the room is the catering area.

"I'm like, 'Oh, sweet. Food.'

"And the security guard goes, 'DON'T EAT ANYTHING!'

"It's like everywhere we went, we weren't supposed to be. It was three months of getting over red tape that we didn't even really want to get over. It was really humiliating, but it was also one of those moments where [we thought], 'The rock gods are testing us. They're asking us if we really want to be here.'"

—*GRACE POTTER,* GRACE POTTER AND THE NOCTURNALS

GILLIAN WELCH

Listeners unfamiliar with the music of singer-songwriter Gillian Welch might conjure an image of her as a gingham-wearing Southerner who grew up in dirt-poor conditions and learned to play guitar from her granpappy. In truth, Welch is a New York City native raised primarily in Los Angeles by parents who cowrote the Emmy-winning musical numbers on The Carol Burnett Show. The Grammy-winning Welch is the poster child for a blend of neo-traditional country and rustic folk, which she dubs "American primitive." The list of performers she's worked with is impressive and eclectic. It's doubtful anyone else can claim to have shared a microphone with Ralph Stanley, Elvis Costello, Norah Jones, Ryan Adams and Bright Eyes.

"In Nashville, before we ever had a record out, I decided I wanted to play this writers' night. I went down there by myself and waited like three or four hours to play. They kept me waiting and kept me waiting as the crowd thinned out. Finally, the guy who had been playing his own songs between every three writers, he got up when there were about three people left and played three more songs. Then he said it was my turn. There was literally nobody left in the place but the bartender and the MC. The MC said, 'OK, you can play now. Will you turn the PA off when you're done?' So I got up and played a couple songs to the bartender, then I walked over and turned the PA off."

—GILLIAN WELCH

GWAR

CREDIT: GIL PEREZ

Satire is rarely so loud. GWAR (purportedly an acronym for "God What an Awful Racket") took shape as a marketing experiment by musicians and art students at Virginia Commonwealth University. The collective concocted an elaborate backstory about alien warriors enslaving the human race, matching it with an equally elaborate stage show characterized by exaggerated latex papier-mâché costumes and simulated graphic violence. Members perform under aliases and behind masks, with singer Oderus Urungus (Dave Brockie) steadfast today as the lone original member. Much to the chagrin of GWAR's critics, the band has seized two Grammy nominations.

$$\bullet \quad \bullet \quad \bullet$$

"The worst place we ever played was in Germany in '93 or so. They'd just knocked down the Wall, and East Germany was just becoming available for metal shows. We played in a town called Halle, in a giant slaughterhouse where apparently there had been some kind of radioactive accident.

"Like any curious creature, as we got to the gig, we started poking around. We found all these lockers full of people's stuff. It looked like they had to leave really fast. Whatever happened had happened recently. It's not like the stuff we found in lockers was from World War II.

"We also found all these photographs of cows—not just living ones—but dead ones being inserted into body bags. First of all, it's a body bag made for a cow; it's a lot bigger than a normal body bag. They're zipping up these cows in bags that have radioactive symbols on them. What are they doing with them? Turning them into hamburger to send to Thailand?

"It was East Germany, so nobody spoke any fucking English or else we would have gotten a better idea what was going on. But we guessed that whatever happened there had happened very quickly. They tried to get it under control. They decided the best thing to do was evacuate the facility. Then metal heads squatted the place because 'no one goes there.' That led to parties, and the local authorities probably didn't care if it was just metal kids.

"We realized the people working in the place were decidedly Mongoloid looking—like something was in the water. As we played, they kind of stood there as if they had witnessed a collective horror.

"We called the place Cowschwitz."

—ODERUS URUNGUS (DAVE BROCKIE), GWAR

THE GET UP KIDS

Platinum-selling acts such as Fall Out Boy and Blink-182 regularly cite The Get Up Kids as their primary influence. The Kansas City quintet—singer-guitarist Matt Pryor, guitarist Jim Suptic, bassist Rob Pope, drummer Ryan Pope and keyboardist James Dewees—became a major component of the emo scene in the mid-1990s. Their 1999 album *Something to Write Home About* remains one of the most acclaimed in the genre. While The Get Up Kids officially broke up in 2005 (with members dispersing to acts such as Spoon and My Chemical Romance), their core lineup reunites occasionally to tour and record, and they released their fifth album, **There Are Rules**, in 2011.

"The Get Up Kids played at Brownies in New York on our very first tour. We rolled up and there were like thirty-five people inside. They were all there to see us. But some band from New Zealand was on the bill, and they actually closed the show. Nobody stuck around to see them, but they had a guarantee so they got *all* the door money. Brownies paid us only $20. We're like, 'We came all the way [from Kansas] to New York and you're going to just hand us a twenty?' So we went into the basement, found out where all the alcohol was stored and stole a bunch of beer. We basically got paid in beer for that show. An 1,100-mile drive for beer."

—*MATT PRYOR*, THE GET UP KIDS

Screamin' Sirens offered a countrified twist on the all-female punk bands that sprung from Hollywood in the late 1970s and mid-1980s. Led by singers Pleasant Gehman and Rosie Flores (and a fairly transient lineup), the group was infamous for its flamboyant live shows and hard-partying offstage antics. Gehman went on to write for Spin *and* LA Weekly, *in addition to writing several books. She's also appeared in a handful of movies, including as the subject of the 2008 documentary* Underbelly, *which focuses on her subsequent career as an international belly-dancing star. She composed this brassy recollection of life on the road.*

TALES OF TOURING TERROR:
THE SCREAMIN' SIRENS' WORST GIG

By Pleasant Gehman

I think it was 1987, and my crazy, liquor-soaked, thrashin' all-girl "cowpunk" band The Screamin' Sirens were on tour promoting our albums *Fiesta* and *Voodoo*. The Sirens were gigging at a roadhouse called Rooster's in Nashville, Tennessee, when this entire chain of events occurred.

Living like full-on *Spinal Tap*–style road pigs, we were in the midst of a self-booked tour, playing every night and, if we were lucky, sleeping on strangers' floors. We traveled in an unheated old Winnebago conversion van, whose ceiling was festooned with fishnet stockings, crepe-paper streamers, bumper stickers and our own lipstick graffiti. The windows on one side of the van were covered with torn-apart Tampax boxes to block out the sun. This story unfolds on the eve of Sirens' bassist Laura's birthday, on a chilly November night.

As twilight fell, I stepped outside the stage door of Rooster's, and as my eyes became accustomed to the dark, I couldn't believe what I was seeing: a mossy Victorian-era gravestone, leaning up against the building in the weeds. There were new dirt and clumps of grass stuck to the bottom of the monument, and it looked to be freshly dug up. Even more amazing, the headstone was for a girl who had died at age twenty-four: the same age Laura was turning that very night. Not only that, the girl had died on Laura's birthday!

Going inside the club to report my find, I asked if there was a graveyard anywhere in the nearby vicinity. Everyone I questioned assured me there was not.

Thinking that the headstone would make the ultimate birthday present, I borrowed a hand truck from the club and cajoled some boys to help get the headstone to our dressing room, then blindfolded Laura and dragged her into the room to see her present. Laura was a tough, hard-drinking, wisecracking punk chick who, before joining the Sirens, had been in a band called Hard as Nails, Cheap as Dirt. She had a macabre sense of humor and, like the rest of us, always appreciated a low-budget splatter flick. So the whole band assumed she'd be delighted with her present, especially since we were too broke to be able to afford anything else.

As her blindfold was removed, instead of the anticipated reaction of laughter, Laura turned white as a ghost (pun intended!) and whispered, her voice trembling audibly, "Get that fucking thing out of here right now!"

Disappointed that our gift didn't go over well, we scrambled to get the gravestone back outside, crashing into amps and drum sets in the narrow hallway on the way outside.

After that, the headstone seemed to put a curse on everything that happened.

Our gig that night was terrible—maybe the worst of the tour, plagued with more than our usual share of technical difficulties. The boys we were flirting with didn't respond the way they usually did, the audience was a bunch of dullard cowboys and we didn't sell any merch.

As we loaded up the van in a dense fog, it began to drizzle. Laura's purse somehow disappeared from the parking lot. The whole band searched for ages both inside and outside the club (as well as in our van), but her purse had vanished without a trace. Then, dead tired and with no speed or even coffee, because it was so late that even rural convenience marts and truck stops weren't open, Laura and I drove the van through pouring torrential rain for three and a half hours before discovering we'd gone in the wrong direction. Usually, we chattered endlessly on our late-night drives, but tonight we were both quiet and grimly introspective. Practically crying, we finally figured out the right way to go.

Back on course, we were speeding through Kentucky at daybreak, desperately trying to get to St. Louis on time for our gig that night, when *of course* we got pulled over.

Laura was driving, and since her purse was missing, she had no license. We both looked completely terrifying—in our previous night's sweat-caked stage makeup, with remnants of glitter crusted around our eyes, we looked like carnival corpses from a cheap fun house. Laura was wearing a decomposing vintage beaver-fur coat over long johns, and I looked like a dead clown: orange hair with rags tied into it, a man's 1950s pajama shirt, a huge torn-up net petticoat, boxer shorts, striped stockings and turquoise Converse high-tops. Everyone else was passed out cold, and we were hoping the van wouldn't get searched, because if it did, we'd probably wind up on a rural chain gang!

The cop didn't even have to say, "Y'ain't from 'round heeere, are ya?"

You could see the diabolical, inbred glint in his eyes. Miraculously, he didn't seem to notice the scores of empty Budweiser cans that littered the floor, along with stray fishnet stockings, crumpled cigarette packs, NoDoz, rolling papers, battered cowboy boots, and an empty bottle of Everclear.

He screwed us up pretty good, anyway: Not only did we get a $75 ticket (an astronomical amount in those days, especially for us), but he held us up for almost forty minutes as he made a huge deal of having his dispatcher call Los Angeles to make sure that Laura didn't have any arrest warrants. The fact that it was confirmed to be her birthday held no sway with him, and even though we explained our predicament—her stolen purse, being late for a gig and the fact that the road we were speeding on was completely deserted—he still almost gleefully wrote us the ticket.

Finally arriving in St. Louis, we sent our entire band

fund back to LA by money order. Our reasoning was that because of the way things had been going, we were scared to keep a big amount of cash with us, in case it got lost or stolen. Plus, our gig that night had the largest guarantee of the tour, so we'd be flush in a matter of hours.

When we got to the club, the booking agent who'd hired us had apparently been fired recently and the new manager was like, "Screaming WHO?!"

We sat in the parking lot forlornly, with grim reality setting in. We had only sixty-odd dollars left to share between seven people—counting our personal monetary stashes—and no gig for three days. As it began to snow, we made repeated attempts to contact the promoter of the next show, in Kansas City, by pay phone, but no dice. Boy, were we bummed.

Pretty soon, the guys in the top-forty house band showed up for their gig that night. Somehow, they found out that we were a stranded all-girl band from LA, and, interest piqued, they smuggled beer and popcorn out to us. We shared our last shreds of pot and told them our tale of woe.

They excitedly told us that Supertramp was playing the Coliseum down the street and that the after-party was being held here at the club—LIKE WE CARED! Supertramp? You must be kidding! We were so "alternative" that we had no idea what Supertramp's hits were—and we didn't give a shit anyway.

But those top-forty guys were being nice to us, so we

were nice right back, acting suitably, charmingly impressed with this "amazing" news.

We borrowed a couple of bucks from them, promising sincerely to send it back from our next gig, and went out to a dismal Italian birthday dinner at the Spaghetti Factory, all of us sharing plates of food, drinking communally from the decanter of hellish cheap red wine. Laura blew out her one candle, and we split a stale chocolate cupcake as though it were manna from heaven. We barely had enough to pay the bill and left someone's key chain and a punk-rock badge as a tip.

We drove back to the club's parking lot (where else were we gonna go, after all?) and figured that since it was really starting to blizzard, and we didn't want to risk driving or running out of gas in a snowstorm, we'd spend the night there in our unheated van.

As if on cue, the top-forty guys came out again with more beer, and we joked around. Even though they were "normal" and we were punk-rock scum, we were still chicks, and *chick musicians* no less—which really was a novelty in those days. They were intrigued by us because, though we were broke and stranded, we were living out a rock-and-roll dream. And besides, we were from HOLLYWOOD!

The guys went inside and convinced the manager to let us play a set on their equipment. They were insanely delighted when we emerged from the bathroom, looking all fresh and newly made up with our garish Ronettes-style eyeliner and Wet N Wild ninety-nine-cent lipstick.

I have to say that we always cleaned up very well, even on tour, with hangovers and no showers. The top-forty guys kept bringing us pitchers of beer before we went on, and while they played, they announced to the entire club that it was Laura's birthday and told our whole sad, crazy story onstage.

Pretty soon the entire club was singing "Happy Birthday" to Laura. We played a wild set, with audience members sending trays of shots to us. Construction workers in plaid shirts were jumping right up onto the stage to shake our hands, steal a kiss, or do a shot with us. The audience was going crazy; they'd apparently never seen five girls in torn-up lingerie and biker jackets jumping around, sweating, cursing and playing well!

Right when we finished, the guys from Supertramp started congratulating us, buying us rounds of cocktails and giving us tons of blow in the dressing room, yelling in English accents about how "FAKKING GREHT!" we were. Then they played and, in between songs, took up a collection from the audience so we could have gas money. We'd played with a wild assortment of bands in our career, from The Ramones to Rosanne Cash, but never thought we'd ever open for Supertramp!

By the end of the night, our roadie had gotten in touch with the promoter in Kansas City and had arranged a place for us to stay that night, which turned out to be his mom's house (soft beds, home-cooked meals, cable television—yee-haw!), so our luck had completely turned around.

It's been decades, but to this day, if you mention the word *birthday* to Laura, she winces in pain and changes the subject right away.

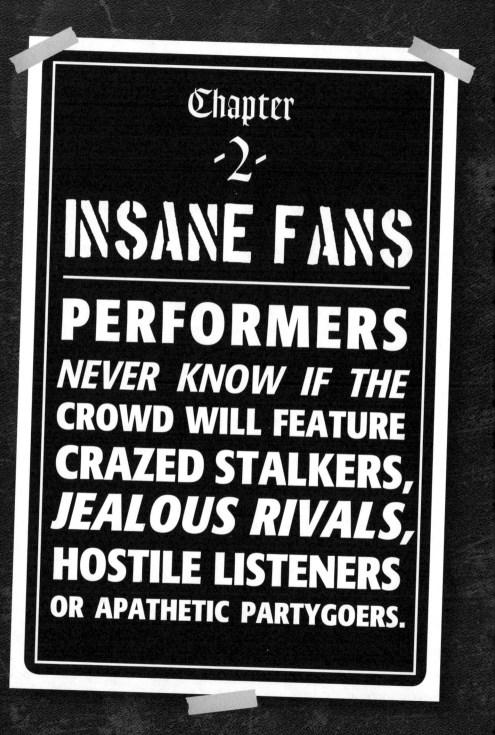

Chapter -2-

INSANE FANS

PERFORMERS NEVER KNOW IF THE CROWD WILL FEATURE CRAZED STALKERS, JEALOUS RIVALS, HOSTILE LISTENERS OR APATHETIC PARTYGOERS.

RUSH

Rush has sold more than forty million records worldwide and garnered untold legions of devoted fans. The Toronto trio was formed in 1968 by high school friends Alex Lifeson and bassist-vocalist Geddy Lee. After an album of basic guitar rock in 1974, the pair brought in replacement drummer Neil Peart, who added his cerebral lyrics and technical prowess to the band's gifted musical mix. In that span, Rush has entrenched its reputation particularly among other performers. Lifeson's densely textured guitar work and eccentric solos, Lee's virtuoso bass riffs and Peart's intricate polyrhythms have influenced the talent of several generations of musicians. Rush was inducted into the Rock and Roll Hall of Fame in 2013.

CREDIT: ANDREW MACNAUGHTAN

"It was a long time ago, the first tour, in fact, in 1974. We were playing at a university in Baltimore. We got to the gig; the crew was setting up. It was just before the show, and we came out to sort of peek around to look at the audience before the doors opened and they came in. And we saw that the girls were dressed in little white socks and long skirts and all the guys had greaser hairdos. It turned out to be one of these '50s sock-hop kind of things. We went on and were wearing satin pants and big high boots. And we started with 'Finding My Way' from the first record. They just sort of stood there and stared at us. Then by the second song they started to rumble. By the fourth song it was 'Booooo! Get out of here! Get off!' So, of course, we turned everything up a little bit and continued to play. Then finally the promoter said, 'That's great. Thanks guys. You're done.' But they were nasty. They were really pissed off. I'm sure if we would have kept going they would have thrown their greasy combs at us."

—*ALEX LIFESON,* RUSH

MUTEMATH

CREDIT: MATT BECHTOLD

Led by the formidable voice and acrobatic keyboard playing of Paul Meany, Mutemath is revered for its engaging live shows. But the band is equally praised for its innovative videos, such as the hit "Typical," a visual gem shot in one unedited take while the group delivers the performance in reverse. Mutemath—often Mute Math, MuteMath, or MUTEMATH—began as a cross-state collaboration between former Earthsuit frontman Meany and drummer Darren King. Eventually, the group expanded into a quartet that settled in New Orleans. The alt-rock act cites numerous influences (many of them British) and has found success ranging from a Grammy nomination to witnessing its material performed by contestants on American Idol.

• • •

"What is it that makes a worst gig? One of the things that's usually a common thread is if you happen to find yourself playing in front of a crowd that does not have any interest in you being on that stage at that particular moment—which is usually when you take opening gigs. Or it's just that gig you need to get from one to the other—it's that middle gig that you have to do. In the early days we found ourselves every now and then getting the chance to open for a very heavy band, which we learned early on is not a good fit for us. If there's too much testosterone in the room, we wilt. I remember we did a gig once in London opening for a band called The Used. To make it even more specific, it was a private party that they were doing for their most diehard fans. So it was the most exclusive, diehard Used fans—there shouldn't have even been an opening band for this kind of thing...I just remember being heckled the whole time. It was just basically high school locker room all over again. The only thing is it was with heavy British accents, so we couldn't understand what was going on. But we knew that they did not like us, and they wanted us to get off the stage as soon as possible...We didn't win anyone over. But we did not relent. We did not just leave the stage. We played our set, as painstaking as it was. We didn't patronize the crowd, either. I don't believe in doing that. We just took it like men, and we moved on and promised ourselves to never open for The Used again."

–PAUL MEANY, MUTEMATH

JULIANA HATFIELD

Originally coming to prominence in the underground Boston trio The Blake Babies and as bassist for The Lemonheads, Juliana Hatfield went solo in 1992 with **Hey Babe,** *the album that first led to her widespread critical acclaim and numerous national magazine cover articles. Subsequently picked up by Atlantic Records, Hatfield issued* **Become What You Are,** *which showcased her "girlie" singing voice, blistering guitar playing and contemplative lyrics via the standout singles "My Sister" and "Spin the Bottle." By the 1995 follow-up* **Only Everything** *(featuring the amiable hit "Universal Heartbeat"), Hatfield had seemingly cornered the college-rock market of radio and MTV.*

"One thing that comes to mind is the show The Blake Babies did in Clemson, South Carolina. We had all cut our hair in a video, then we all shaved our heads just to even it out. We played down in Clemson, and the crowd was giving us so much hell. It was packed with frat guys and drunk people. They were so obnoxious and rude, yelling 'dykes' at us. It was just constant antagonism. But there's something invigorating about fighting against injustice. I think I dumped a beer on some guy's head. We were such snotty punks—not punks in the traditional sense—we just were pretty tough about it. We forged ahead and realized there were at least a few people who got it."

—JULIANA HATFIELD

AFTER THE FIRE

CREDIT: CHRIS COOKE

"Don't turn around, uh-oh / Der Kommissar's in town, uh-oh." London's After the Fire notched a top-five hit with their 1983 cover of Falco's "Der Kommissar," with English lyrics crafted by the band's singer-bassist Andy Piercy. The song proved inescapable during the fledgling days of MTV and catapulted the act to stadium tours with Van Halen and Queen.

◆ ◆ ◆

"We were playing in a small cellar club in the West Side of London. We'd played there a few times, and we thought we'd built a good clientele and interest. We were on one night, and it was quite late. People had been drinking. We'd been doing these songs and playing our hearts out. They were cheering away. But when the cheering died down, they'd start chanting, 'Rub-bish. Rub-bish. Rub-bish.'

"It really upset us. So we'd play the next song harder and faster, and they'd cheer like crazy, then the shouting would start again, 'Rub-bish. Rub-bish. Rub-bish.'

"We were getting really mad. We played the last songs to finish the set, and the shouting kept getting louder each time. We were playing harder and faster to try to win them over. The more we did, the more they shouted.

"We got to the end, and we were so cross that we cut the last song short and left the stage. We didn't have a crew in those days—this was the late '70s—so we had to go out with a sound guy and put everything away in this club. The crowd was still out there.

"One guy said, 'Why didn't you come out and play more?'

"I said, 'Well, you were shouting "Rubbish."'

"He said, 'No we weren't. We were shouting *Rapid*.'

"What was happening was they loved it when we played fast. So they just wanted us to play faster. 'Rapid' was some little foible they'd developed that they thought was real fun.

"We were so mad. One of the best gigs we'd ever done we thought was the worst gig we'd ever had. We were furious.

"The funny result: This was in the old days where After the Fire was a prog-rock band with lots of time changes and long pieces and fiddly stuff. We set up our own indie label and did an album. We called our label Rapid Records."

—ANDY PIERCY, AFTER THE FIRE

INXS

Launched in 1977 in Sydney, Australia, INXS went on to sell thirty million albums. While in the 1980s the dance-friendly rock band dominated MTV and commercial radio with hits such as "Don't Change," "What You Need," "Devil Inside" and "Never Tear Us Apart," it enjoyed a more contemporary boost in 2005 as the centerpiece of the CBS series Rock Star: INXS. The reality competition show provided the members (Jon Farriss, Tim Farriss, Andrew Farriss, Gary Beers and Kirk Pengilly) an opportunity to find a permanent replacement for frontman Michael Hutchence, who died in 1997. Canadian J. D. Fortune was crowned the winner, and his good looks and brooding antics helped INXS return to the charts.

"I do remember in the mid-'80s we supported Queen in Europe for a bunch of shows at Wembley Stadium. We were one of the opening acts. Throughout the whole performance the Queen fans were very 'devout.' They threw all sorts of things at us: cans to bottles to loaves of bread. We had to have our wits about us to dodge the stuff. Even the bread."

—KIRK PENGILLY, INXS

MIKE WATT

CREDIT: CARL JOHNSON

Mike Watt has earned the tag of the hardest-working man in underground rock. The punk-rock legend is responsible for the booming bass guitar and voice that has powered Minutemen, Firehose, Dos and numerous solo projects for more than three decades. He's also lent his four-string skills to live tours with Porno for Pyros and the reunited Stooges. But those are just a fraction of the collaborations enjoyed by this jovial performer who is known for his blend of punk energy and working-class earnestness.

♦ ♦ ♦

"There was a Minutemen gig where we got booted from the club during the soundcheck. It was the Cuckoo's Nest. There was a new owner or some shit—we had played there before. We were sound-checking with 'Joy,' a song that's not even a minute long. This owner looked around and said, 'You guys sound like *that*? I thought you played the Roxy?' Then he just started laughing at us and said, 'Pack it up, boys.'

"I also remember the first time we got into the Whisky [a Go Go] with Fear, and then X asked us to open up. We got the chance to play at the Croatian Hall, so we were like, 'We'll open up for them at 7:30, then we'll rush back to San Pedro to play.'

"I'd just had knee surgery, so I was doing the fucking gig in a chair with my leg in a cast. We got down there, and it was like, 'Wow. A club with monitors. You can actually hear.'

"Then we rushed back [to the Whisky] and it was a bunch of jocks dancing to new-wave stuff. By the time it was our turn to go on, it was maybe one or two songs before they started throwing things. First it was just the ice in the drinks. Then it was the glasses. I couldn't dodge. I'm in a chair in a cast, and I'm getting hit with all this shit. Then somebody pulls the power and shut the whole thing off.

"We also had this gig in Vienna. It was the first time Minutemen played over there. It was with Black Flag. The first note of the first song, all the power goes off. It comes back on, and I've got a dozen used condoms thrown all over me. They're hanging on my neck, on my shirt. [Guitarist] D. Boon got hit in the face with a cup of piss.

"We call those kinds of gigs character builders. But the ones where we got stopped and couldn't play anymore, those are really the worst gigs. They're failures because we don't get to finish."

—MIKE WATT

RUFUS WAINWRIGHT

The son of folk singers Kate McGarrigle and Loudon Wainwright III, Rufus Wainwright was already touring with his mom, aunt and sister by his early teens. While Wainwright certainly inherited his wry humor and lyrical skills from his parents, the style of music he chose to pursue proved quite dissimilar. The Canadian singer-pianist has established a bridge between commercial-pop songwriting and sophisticated theatrical orchestration. That coupled with his dramatic, vibrato-heavy voice has made the performer a unique commodity in the industry.

"It might have been one of those Lisa Loeb shows [where I was the opener]. I think it was in Tucson, Arizona, and I just stopped in the middle and said, 'Good night, fuckers!' and walked offstage. They wouldn't stop talking and were very much into screaming—grunting, I should say—'Lisa, Lisa, Lisa.' I think it was because the boyfriends had gone to the show with their girlfriends, who had thus promised certain sexual favors if they would go to this show. They just weren't into it. And they weren't into an opening act—especially a little gay boy from Canada."

—RUFUS WAINWRIGHT

TENACIOUS D

Originally conceived as the basis for an HBO comedy series in 1999, the "band" Tenacious D is the brainchild of actor-musicians Jack Black and Kyle Gass—two of the most unlikely rock stars to ever strap on six-strings. The wild-eyed Black is a household name for his leads in the films **The School of Rock** and **Kung Fu Panda.** The bald Gass has had cameos in several movies but is perhaps best known for being the less talkative foil of Tenacious D. The pair's abrasive comedy spawns from their being two acoustic guitar players so convinced that their music is the very definition of stadium rock that they berate and mock all those who can't perceive their rightful glory.

"We opened for Pearl Jam. We opened for Weezer. We also opened for Tool, which was a huge mistake we made over and over again—three times. They were too hardcore. The audience was very angry at us for being us…They didn't want a joke. You don't go to Tool to laugh. You go to be angry and vent…I can't remember what they were throwing, but we definitely got pelted. We tried to play our hardest-rocking songs, but it never mixed."

—JACK BLACK, TENACIOUS D

BETTIE SERVEERT

Formed in 1990 in Amsterdam, the group Bettie Serveert took its name from an instruction manual by Dutch tennis star Betty Stove. Translation: "Bettie serves." Between 1992 and 1997, the sometimes jangly, sometimes gritty ensemble released three signature albums—Palomine, Lamprey and Dust Bunnies—which cemented its reputation in the college-rock scene. Years on the road with acts such as Dinosaur Jr., Buffalo Tom, Superchunk and Counting Crows helped buoy its indie fan base. While various drummers have come and gone, the core membership of Carol van Dyk (vocals and guitar), Peter Visser (guitar) and Herman Bunskoeke (bass) has remained solid through nine albums.

"There's a very small festival in Holland. It's called—translated in English—Easter Pop. It's the worst festival you'd ever want to play. It's infamous for that. Most people are completely drunk by 2 p.m.…It's in the middle of farm country in Holland. They get so completely wasted that it doesn't really matter what's onstage as long as they can sort of jump to it. There are only a couple of bands, specifically Dutch singing bands, who can play there and get away with it without getting bombarded. It's not because they hate the bands; it's just because they're so drunk that they don't really care. It's usually rolls of toilet paper that they throw, for no apparent reason. We've only done the festival once. And we came offstage and were like, 'Never again!'"

—*CAROL VAN DYK,* BETTIE SERVEERT

CREDIT: DIANE BONEBRAKE

One of America's most acclaimed punk bands, X was part of the first-wave pack to emerge on the LA club scene in 1977. The visually distinctive act was aided early on by former Doors keyboardist Ray Manzarek, who produced the 1980 debut LP **Los Angeles** *and the follow-up* **Wild Gift.** *Powered by the atypical harmonies of singers John Doe and Exene Cervenka, the quartet (including guitarist Billy Zoom and drummer DJ Bonebrake) brought punk's raging tempos together with rockabilly and roots influences.*

◆ ◆ ◆

"It was the Elks' Lodge in 1979 in LA, and we were headlining. The Go-Go's were on before us, and The Alley Cats—might have been The Plugz…While The Go-Go's were playing, somebody called the cops, and about two hundred cops came to the site and broke the concert up.

"I was sitting out in the lobby. Nothing was going on, and I was bored. Then suddenly the cops show up and boot us out. There were cops outside in formation. There were helicopters. There were snipers. It was like, 'What was going on?' *The Go-Go's* were playing.

"They pushed everyone down the street. We were crying foul. 'Why are you doing this?'

"There were no riots. But some of the kids smashed a police car. Someone I knew got thrown in jail. I actually loaned her money to bail her out. It was in the news, these rioting punks. So a lot of the punk rockers went on AM radio and defended us.

"What I heard is that a couple of the kids went into a wedding ceremony or wedding party, and they disrupted it somewhat. So I guess that's a reason to call the police, but maybe not two hundred police. That was the rumor. I never got to the bottom of it. I should try to investigate what really happened...I wasn't in a position to do that thirty years ago.

"In a way that was the worst gig because we never got to play.

"Another one I can remember happened to me but it wasn't with X. I was playing [in] Oslo with Dave Alvin. We played two nights in 1991, and the first night the Gulf War started...But the next night we played and were about five songs into our set, and our road manager comes onstage and says, 'Don't ask any questions. Just stop playing!'

"So we leave, and they announce that the king of Norway had just died and the gig was canceled. Some people were respectful, and other people were going, 'Fuck the king.' We got the info that there was no music allowed until further notice."

–DJ BONEBRAKE, X

Vocalist-guitarist Rick Valentin, bassist Rose Marshack, guitarist Jim Valentin and many drummers have kept Poster Children humming along the indie-rock highway since 1987. With an impeccable reputation for do-it-yourself ethics and immersive live shows, the foursome from Champaign, Illinois, is also lauded for its groundbreaking use of technology (blogs, podcasts and enhanced CDs) when promoting its music. Marshack culled this tale from her extensive tour journals.

POSTER CHILDREN'S
COLORFUL ARRAY OF CRAPPY GIGS

By Rose Marshack

Poster Children don't really have worst gigs (and actually, we don't play "gigs," we play "shows"). We have what we call learning experiences. The Dalai Lama once said, "In the practice of tolerance, one's enemy is the best teacher," and we extrapolated from this: There are no bad shows, only learning experiences.

Throughout our vast continuum of twenty-five years of learning experiences in the United States and Europe, a few stand out. Most of the time it is easy to distinguish the lesson from the experience. For example, there was the time in Portland, Maine, where I couldn't finish the show because I got food poisoning.

Playing with Public Enemy in Lawrence, Kansas, [in] 1992, was a serious learning experience. Public Enemy had just performed with Sonic Youth in Chicago, so we figured it would be OK, and since we liked Sonic Youth, we figured there'd be some audience crossover. So we were slightly surprised, and educated, when one thousand white college students stood in front of us as we played, screaming, "GET OFF THE STAGE!" [and] holding up their tickets with their fingers covering up the words *opening act.*"

CREDIT: JAMIE KELLY

We took a vote to see how many of them would rather hear silence for the next forty-five minutes (that was another learning experience) and then replied with "Too BAD!" and played "If You See Kay" probably way too fast, but it had to have been fun for Rick to scream into his mic at that point. Public Enemy, by the way, were very complimentary after we played, although Flavor Flav had missed our set and was a half hour late for his own because, as he said, he'd lost his clock.

Then there was a show where we asked Urge Overkill if we could play with them in Madison, Wisconsin. They said yes, but they made us play before the doors opened. One time we mistakenly arrived at Gabe's Oasis in Iowa City, Iowa, a day early. When the woman at the bar told me we weren't playing that night, I just started crying. I also cried, onstage, when I accidentally broke my Travis Bean bass in half, playing in Gainesville, Florida. Twice, our van caught on fire on the way to a show. Then there was our first time in New York City—we'd driven all the way from Illinois— and I entered the club and proudly stated, "Hello! We're Poster Children! We're playing here tonight!" And the man behind the bar answered loudly, "So?"

But, by far, the best learning experience we ever had was playing to three thousand people in Detroit, Michigan, at an outdoor radio festival. We were sandwiched between The Smithereens, who were headlining, and Prong, who probably *should* have been headlining. Any band should know that playing a festival is a stupid move, but this was early in our career and for some reason, we had agreed to do it. "You'll get added to the radio station if you play," I'm sure we were told.

I remember being on the stage for a soundcheck, scrambling around to finish within the allotted fifteen minutes between the leather heroes and the geezers, when, looking for an outlet to plug into, I asked a stagehand, "Excuse me, where is the power?" He looked at me and replied, "I'll take 'no-name bands' for $50."

Fuming, I found the outlet myself, plugged my amp in and marched up to the front of the stage—only to find that my guitar cable was not even long enough to reach from the back line to the front of the stage. Yoink! We had to move all the amps up. Humiliating.

Leather-clad Prong went on the stage and probably began to play some B-minor chords really quickly and loudly as the audience filled in. I can't even imagine how upset they had to have been about opening the show. Then their fans jumped out of the assigned seating and rushed to the stage, raising their hands and fists and singing along with the band. The stage manager was horrified—and terrified. "We can't have people out of their seats during the show DANCING?!" he cried. He motioned to the security men. "Cut the power! Cut the power!" The power went dead. Poor Prong had no more electricity, only black leather and drums—and they were not happy

The fans were not amused, either. "Prong!!" they shouted angrily. "PRONG!! PRONG!!" And then some fans jumped onto the stage. At this point, Rick and I were staring at the crowd, horrified. We were pretty sure that anyone who might have been even remotely interested in seeing us were at a Smashing Pumpkins revival show down at the other side of town, and I was worried the Prong fans wanted to beat us up even before the show started—or at least hold up their tickets with our name crossed off them. All of a sudden, the terrified stage crew started yelling, "We're calling the riot police! We're calling the riot police!" The next thing we knew, Detroit's finest riot police, complete with helmets and weapons, had formed a semicircle in front of the stage. The power was still out, kids were shouting, "PRONG!! PRONG!! PRONG!!" and filing out of the canopy.

"SET UP YOUR EQUIPMENT!" the manager told me. "AND IF ANY-ONE GETS OUT OF THEIR SEATS DURING YOUR SHOW, YOUR SET WILL BE OVER," he threatened.

I stood up and looked at the remainder of the audience. The front thousand seats were emptying out. "WE DEDICATE THIS SET TO PRONG," I yelled.

I'd never even met Prong, but, man, did I feel bad for them. And so we played—ferociously and then angrily and self-righteously to show the Detroit riot police, The Smithereens and the waning crowd ("This isn't Prong anymore, right?") just how punk rock we were. And then Rick lobbed his Musicmaster guitar (complete with American flag sticker) over the riot police's head, straight into the audience, where a lucky crowd member came to, grabbed the guitar and ran off with it. The riot police held their ground in front of the stage to protect us from the crowd, who were leaving in droves by that time.

Touring for twenty-five years was wonderful—every last minute of it. I'd do it all again. Turn your prisons into playgrounds, The Situationists said. And so we did. And so should you.

Chapter -3-

DANGEROUS MALFUNCTIONS

FAULTY STAGES, SUSPECT ELECTRONICS AND ANTAGONISTIC PROPS ARE A FEW OF THE THINGS THAT CAN GO AMISS AT A LIVE SHOW—AND THAT'S JUST THE BEGINNING.

FLAMING LIPS

Since emerging in 1983, Flaming Lips—singer-guitarist Wayne Coyne, multi-instrumentalist Steven Drozd, bassist Michael Ivins and drummer Kliph Scurlock—have been rock's go-to act for genre-pushing reinventions. The Oklahoma City group remains one of the rare bands to master both the studio and the live stage with equal acclaim, complementing its Grammy-winning music with elaborate costumes, puppets, mounds of confetti and Coyne's man-sized plastic bubble in which he navigates across the audience.

◆ ◆ ◆

"There's always some catastrophe that we think in our minds is ruining it for everybody, then a lot of times people don't even notice. But we were playing at a not-that-great-of-a-little festival, opening up for Cake and playing with Modest Mouse in 2002 or something like that. We were playing at Red Rocks, the big prestigious venue in Denver, Colorado, to a sold-out crowd of about ten thousand people. We were working on our smoke machine backstage, and it kept triggering a fuse, blowing the electricity.

"We're there all day fucking with our gear and all that, and I went to one of the technicians at the place and said, 'This is blowing a fuse here. I'm worried that when we go onstage we're going to blow the electricity.'

"He laughed and said, 'Look, dude, we had Slayer play here. Give me a fucking break.'

"I said, 'We've played places where Slayer has played a lot, and it's just kind of ramshackle.'

"I put it to the back of my mind. That having been said, we go onstage, the smoke machine goes, and the fucking whole place blows. The whole place. We stand in the dark apologizing best we can because there're no fucking microphones [working]. The electricity comes back on, and we say, 'Sorry about that. We'll trudge on.'

"Two minutes later, bam, the electricity goes out again. I see this guy who told me Slayer played there, and I'm like, 'Dude, it's just a fucking smoke machine. It's not like we're [Nikola] Tesla trying to get our coil to reignite the stratosphere.'

"Again we trudge on, and when the electricity comes back on we apologize best we can. And it happens yet a third time.

"At some point we've used up the allotted forty-five minutes for our set just with them mucking around trying to get us working again. And yet it's not really humiliating. You just stand there and think, 'Fuck, we want to present this show and you wanted to see it, and this moment has been messed up by people not being prepared.'

"But I have to say I've run into people who saw us at that show since then, and didn't even know who we were because they came to see some of the other bands, and [they] said, 'You stood there, and just seeing you stand there trying to make this work, I really loved you guys.'

"You never know if it's the music you're playing or the way the light hits you…You never know what it is that lets the moment become magical. So I welcome all the calamities that come with performing. Sometimes within the disaster is that elusive magic."

—WAYNE COYNE, FLAMING LIPS

DWEEZIL ZAPPA

Virtuoso guitarist Dweezil Zappa is obliged to respond to two questions his whole life: Yes, that's his real name. And yes, his dad is Frank Zappa, one of rock's greatest musician-composers. Whether releasing his own solo albums, guesting on other people's records, or attempting to honor the music of his late father through the Zappa Plays Zappa act, Dweezil is an industrious guitarist and frontman.

"With Zappa Plays Zappa we really haven't played a bad show because everybody is so focused on doing the best job possible. If we're going to give ourselves a hard time and say it wasn't a good show, it's still far better than a lot of other things. We never go up there and have a total train wreck. You might miss a few parts here and there, but that's because they're fucking hard. Outside of that…I generally try not to get involved in things that I don't like…We've had things that have happened that you can't control. Like we played in Roanoke, Virginia—I'm pretty sure that's where it was—and we played one song, and I stepped on my volume pedal to turn it down so I could change guitars. Then the next song starts and I have no sound. I'm thinking maybe a cable or something is weird. Forty-five minutes later, I still have no guitar sound. At that point we have techs onstage, and I've been conducting the band and doing stuff. But we finally had to resort to putting on house music for a minute while we're completely taking apart my guitar system. Come to find out what it was is there's a little thread in the volume pedal that is part of the mechanism that when you turn it on or off this thread is involved. And it snapped, leaving it stuck in the off position. That's the last thing you think of when it comes to 'let's find the problem.' Forty-five minutes later that was, 'Well, let's look at the volume pedal.' We had that little forty-five-minute snafu, then we played for another two hours after we got it fixed."

—DWEEZIL ZAPPA

UME

CREDIT: MATT BECHTOLD

Ume (pronounced "oo-may") first earned raves from Rolling Stone in 2011 as one of the nation's best unsigned bands. Now the trio from Austin, Texas, is touring on its sophomore LP, Phantoms, which showcases the intricate guitar chops and ethereal vocals of frontwoman Lauren Larson. The road-savvy indie band, which also includes bassist Eric Larson (Lauren's husband) and drummer Rachel Fuhrer, evokes comparisons to Blonde Redhead, Metric and Sonic Youth through its mesh of textural melodies and anthemic hard rock. Ume was recently featured on an episode of **Anthony Bourdain: No Reservations**, *taking the host on a tour of Austin eateries.*

◆ ◆ ◆

"We have a van curse, where literally—I hate to say it—we are tens of thousands of dollars in debt from the van. The first van we ever bought was $400, and we got it at a salvage auction in Pennsylvania, where I was going to school. We didn't even know if it was going to run. I don't know why we bid on it. It had a rusted-out bottom. We'd taken it all the way to the West Coast. It broke down four times—blew a head gasket in the Mojave Desert. That was pretty bad. But then we had twenty bucks, and I ended up going to Vegas, renting a car, turning that $20 into $80…it was on a nickel slot called Filthy Rich.

"Then we had another van and ended up putting a new engine in it. We booked a tour…We've always done preventative maintenance. We didn't even get eight miles out of Austin. We broke down in the middle of the freeway after we'd already had to replace the engine.

"Then we ended up borrowing our friend's diesel, which had 450,000 miles. That could have taken him to the moon. So we said, 'Let's get a diesel van.'

"We get the diesel van, and it's broken down every single tour.

"When I broke down in Nebraska this last time [in 2011], it was like this big rodeo day. [The people at the repair shop] were going, 'Well, we're gonna close at noon. It's Rodeo Days.'

"I was like, 'I don't know what that is.'

"So I had to put on my country-girl accent: 'Could someone work a miracle for me today? We're on the road from Texas.'

"He's like, 'All right. Let me see what I can do.'

"They ended up taking our van in. We made it to the show. We ran onstage, plugged into someone else's gear, played one song, and the stage manager was like, 'You're done!'"

—LAUREN LARSON, UME

RENAISSANCE

London's Renaissance organized in 1969 as a folk-rock project for two ex-Yardbirds, kicking around England's campus circuit with little fanfare. It wasn't until 1973's **Ashes Are Burning** that the ensemble became a mainstay on the English progressive-rock circuit, showcasing orchestral arrangements and extended instrumentals. The album also established the band's core duo, guitarist Michael Dunford and singer Annie Haslam, whose pristine yet ethereal voice boasts a five-octave range.

"We were driving along this highway in Pennsylvania, and we looked over at a truck stop and saw this yellow truck in the lake. It was on an incline, I guess, and it went over. So we had a good laugh about that and thought, 'Thank God, it's not ours.' We'd had the whole day before we were to play Penn State, and we'd stopped for lunch and did whatever—there was a lot of time before the show. But anyway, when we eventually got to the venue, all the equipment was lying out on the grass drying. That *was* our truck in the lake…A [roadie] had parked the truck and put the hand brake on, and obviously the hand brake failed. Don't remember if the truck had our instruments in it, but it had speakers and our whole PA—we usually had more than one truck. We didn't think we'd be able to do the gig, but we did."

—*ANNIE HASLAM*, RENAISSANCE

YUNG SKEETER

Trevor McFedries transformed from a rural Iowa football star to LA producer and performer Yung Skeeter in record time. While teamed with Shwayze and Cisco Adler, he became the first DJ to perform during the entire Vans Warped Tour in 2008. Well respected for his live sets and remixes, Skeeter (formerly known as DJ Skeet Skeet) was recently on the road with Katy Perry on her California Dreams tour, exposing audiences to material such as his signature single "I Like It Loud."

◆ ◆ ◆

"**T**he most memorable was one of my first really big DJ gigs. I had a show in Las Vegas, and I totally stressed myself out about it. Basically, I got to the gig, checked my emails and I had a problem with the booking agent because I had a gig the next day in Orange County that was about as big. So I scrambled, bought myself a flight ticket and got that happening. I ended up losing a ton of money because the flight cost more than both gigs combined were worth. But I just knew I had to be there.

"I do the gig in Vegas and feel great about it. I got to the airport and decided to work on some things for the next gig that was happening that day. I had an external hard drive that I would work off of. I put it between my laptop computer screen and my keyboard, and then I dropped something. So I reached over to grab it and smashed my screen against my external hard drive, and it basically wrecked this computer screen. So I couldn't use my laptop for my

DJ set. I basically called every friend I had and asked them if I could borrow their computer so I could copy all my music over, all my sets. I ended up using my buddy's laptop.

"I copied everything over, reinstalled the software with seconds to spare. Got onstage at this proper nightclub gig with one thousand kids or so there looking at me. I start playing a song, and I'm feeling good. 'This is going to be great. It actually worked out.' And I realize I had set both the channels' 'out' on the software to the same side of the mixer. Basically, I couldn't mix songs.

"It was one of those situations where I was like, 'What am I gonna do now?' I had to wing forty-five minutes of me playing a song, starting a song, looping it out, bringing another song in, talking on the mic.

"I'm sure a whole roomful of kids thought I was an amateur whack job. It was pretty dreadful. It was forty-five minutes of me looking at my clock: 'How can I get off of here?'"

—YUNG SKEETER

OTEP

Otep (an anagram for poet, although the singer insists, "That's my real name") fronts the Los Angeles–based group of the same moniker. She gained her reputation by being one of the lone female voices on the male-centric Ozzfest tour. The vocalist is comfortable growling, whispering, lecturing and rapping her way through topics laced with virulent feminism and peppered with shards of ancient imagery.

"There was a time on Ozzfest [in 2001] where a lot of things went wrong. We had two guitar players who are no longer in the band. I had to release them from the band because they had lost focus of my vision. One of the guys couldn't get his gear working, and he couldn't get his amps going. He didn't understand why nothing was coming out of his guitar. We were fifteen minutes into our set time, so we only had five minutes left to play. The reason was he had forgotten to turn the amp on! Prior to this, he was an electrician by trade."

—OTEP

BELLE AND SEBASTIAN

Although actor Jack Black famously described Belle and Sebastian as "old sad bastard music" in the movie **High Fidelity,** *audiences and critics have been charmed by the band's "wistful chamber pop" for years. Formed in Glasgow, Scotland, in 1996, the act's reclusive approach helped foster a major cult following. After a several-year hiatus, the band is touring and recording again, with a lineup that includes singer-guitarist Stuart Murdoch, guitarist Stevie Jackson, violinist Sarah Martin, keyboardist Chris Geddes, drummer Richard Colburn, bassist Bob Kildea and multi-instrumentalist Mick Cooke.*

◆ ◆ ◆

"It was Manchester Town Hall in 1997. The band hadn't been going very long, maybe a year or so. We always had mad ideas. We had one where we would be onstage in the middle—like in a boxing ring—with the audience surrounding us. But the whole thing with being onstage is the band is listening through monitors; the audience is listening through speakers. That's the classic performance model in the technical sense. What you hear and what the audience hears is completely different.

"When we started we always preferred playing cafes. Small places. Even at an acoustic bar with a very small vocal PA, you can get the sense if you angle things in a way that you're experiencing the same thing. It gives it more of a communal feeling to the experience. Our idea was to get that same experience.

"But this was not a cafe; it's a town hall. There

were maybe 1,000 or even 1,200 people. We had two stages. The band members were offset in the center with people surrounding us. Then there was another island in the back of the room where the keyboards were…And there were speakers facing in on us—this being the idea that the audience and the band were going to hear exactly the same thing. This was the concept.

"It was a complete disaster.

"We were all playing out of sync with each other, especially the keyboards, because they were in a different part of the room. [From] what I could hear, I could tell it was the worst gig I'd ever been to. I was just going, 'This is utterly dreadful.' It was back in the days before computers, and Chris [Geddes] had a real Mellotron. It was completely out of tune.

"Performing at this was a huge nightmare. And then later in Manchester I found out Johnny Marr [of The Smiths] was at the gig. He was there to witness the worst band ever. My worst gig was probably one of the worst gigs in popular music history.

"But I think it looked pretty good."

—STEVIE JACKSON, BELLE AND SEBASTIAN

WILCO

Jeff Tweedy was a founding member of the influential alt-country act Uncle Tupelo. But his follow-up project, Wilco, has proved far more durable and successful than his formative band. Only singer-guitarist Tweedy and bassist John Stirratt have remained with Wilco since its formation in 1994, witnessing more than a dozen members come and go. The unifying factor that has kept the Chicago quintet centered through years of experimentation and internal turbulence is Tweedy's inimitable Grammy-winning songwriting.

"It's a tie. There are two. The Sasquatch Festival in 2004 with this [current] lineup of the band. We went on after Arcade Fire, which is kind of hard to do anyway. They had so many instruments that the monitor lines were crossed. We had a hopeless monitor situation. It was completely messed up on the monitor front. Not only did we have no monitors, we [also] had really strange sampled sounds coming back at us at a huge volume. That was the most disconcerting show I've ever played. That was the most uncomfortable hour onstage ever. I saw it on YouTube. It actually sounded pretty good—he had everything coming out front. But it's a very uncomfortable-looking band onstage. We also did a festival in Indiana in 1995. The first record had just come out and we hadn't toured much, and we had no concept [of] how to get sound through a festival stage with monitors. There was a lightning storm. I remember it was the most ham-fisted live gig ever. We couldn't blame youth either. We weren't really that young. It's hard when there's nobody to pass the buck to."

—*JOHN STIRRATT,* WILCO

An erstwhile member of Jellyfish, The Three O'Clock and The Grays, journeyman Jason Falkner eventually found his songwriting and performing niche as a solo artist. His 1996 debut Jason Falkner Presents Artist Unknown *represents one of the essential power-pop efforts of the era. Whether producing, arranging, or contributing various instruments to albums by artists such as Paul McCartney and Beck, the Los Angeles musician displays a mastery of many talents.*

THE FRENCH-ISH CONNECTION

By Jason Falkner

There are various reasons a gig can go south. In my experience it can start with the venue itself. Nothing nearby to eat except a 7-Eleven hot dog, no stall doors in the bathroom, grounding problems and/or spilt beer on the stage floor resulting in electrocution every time your lips touch the microphone. The list goes on.

My particular worst gig happened in the lovely city of Paris, France. I was flown there to do some solo shows at what I was told was a very authentic Parisian club that also served traditional French cuisine. In other words, it was supposed to be *happening.*

It turned out to be a touristy Hard Rock Cafe–type bummer.

I brought three guitars with me—all vintage and worth way more than your average road guitar. I should've known things weren't gonna go my way when the record company guy left all three guitars in the trunk of the cab he was

following me to the gig in. After a full-blown panic attack and several calls to the car agency, the driver returned with my babies minutes before I was supposed to take the stage.

At this time in my career [1998], I was doing a lot of solo electric guitar shows and had just started using some of my instrumental (nonvocal) mixes onstage. I had a Discman (RIP), and I would do a few songs late in my set with the instrumental tracks as my backup band. Hey, I thought it was cool.

So I enter this joint and climb onstage, and all I can say is that the clatter of cutlery and conversation is louder than the PA speakers. *A lot* louder. I start my show with my acoustic guitar. Things are going well, and the people seem to be enjoying what I'm doing enough to take less frequent bites. This gets me a little excited, and I start jumping around (during this solo show era of mine I would often pretend there was a band behind me), at which point my foot becomes entangled with my guitar cord and the jack rips out from the back of the guitar during a particularly spastic move.

So now I grab my electric and usher in the backing CD portion of my show. After a couple of songs, people are shouting for me to go back to the acoustic (probably because it was less of an assault). I ignore this request, of course, because my acoustic is broken! So I'm rocking out, and then my strap rips where it connects to the front strap pin.

Holy shit, what else can go wrong?

I pick up the acoustic and do my last couple of songs with no amplification, and perhaps because dinner service has ended, people seem to be paying attention and rooting for me. I finish the last song with a bang and lift my guitar above my head to take a bow...and the crowd goes completely bananas!

I'm standing there amazed at this reaction when I look down in horror to see that my willy has exited my accidentally unzipped trousers.

Now *that* is a finale. *Vive la France!*

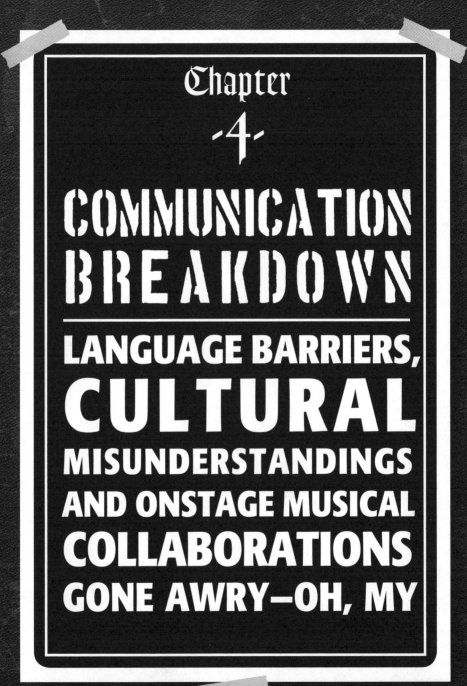

Chapter
-4-

COMMUNICATION BREAKDOWN

LANGUAGE BARRIERS, CULTURAL MISUNDERSTANDINGS AND ONSTAGE MUSICAL COLLABORATIONS GONE AWRY—OH, MY

FLOGGING MOLLY

CREDIT: MATT BECHTOLD

Few bands have blended two seemingly unrelated styles more successfully than Flogging Molly, a rollicking mix of traditional Irish music and punk rock. Dublin native Dave King had established himself as the lead singer of 1980s metal act Fastway when in 1993 he decided to team up with some friends for a weekly gig at LA pub Molly Malone's. Eventually, the lineup became permanent, featuring fiddle player (and King's future wife) Bridget Regan, guitarist Dennis Casey, accordion player Matt Hensley, drummer George Schwindt, bassist Nathen Maxwell and mandolinist Bob Schmidt. Flogging Molly continues to enjoy an unusually loyal following, which celebrates the band's poetic collision of Old World and New World sounds.

◆ ◆ ◆

"One of my horrible touring experiences was in… the United Kingdom. We were on the bus, and you can't take a shit on your bus. So when you stop at a truck stop, that's when you have to do your business. We were driving, and I had one of those times when I woke up and 'you got to go.' There are no questions. I won't get into too much detail. We've all had the experience.

"I got to run off the bus because it just stopped. Perfect. I threw on my shorts and my flip-flops, and I run into the gas station. I do my business. I come out and the bus isn't there. I go, 'Oh, they probably went around back because they were in front.' I walk around back. The bus isn't there. I walk around front again. The bus isn't there.

"I don't have a cell phone. I don't have any money. I don't have any ID. I have nothing but shorts and flip-flops. Now I'm at this British truck stop. It's eight in the morning. I'm hung over, and I look like shit. I realize the bus has left me, and I don't know what to do. With cell phones—I'm sure people can relate to this—you don't memorize numbers anymore. The first thing was like, 'I'll call somebody.' But I don't remember any-body's number! But it doesn't matter because I don't have a cell phone or any money for a pay phone.

"I walk in [to the gas station], and this grumpy old lady is behind the [counter]. I said, 'I gotta ask you a favor.' I ask her, 'Can I call the U.S.?'

"She's like, 'Piss off. No, you can't use our phone.'

"I was like, 'But I really have to.'

"She was not having any of that.

"I walk out and there's a hotel across the street. I walk over and ask, 'Can I use your phone to call the U.S.? I was left by my tour.'

"They just look at you like you're out of your mind—drugs or whatever they're thinking. I'm des-perately trying to be calm and cool about it.

"They're like, 'No. No. No.'

"I'm panicking now. I'm walking around and walk-ing around. By the way, we have laminates on the tour that tell you where your next city is. I didn't have my laminate. So I couldn't tell anybody where I was going either. I don't keep track of that—you show up and you're there.

"I go to [another] gas station. They're like, 'No. Can't use the phone. Sorry, buddy.'

"I'm just walking around. An hour goes by. I'm panicked. 'What am I gonna do? I don't know where I have to go. I don't have any money, no cell phone, nobody's number. I'm in the middle of England, and I don't even know where I am in England to tell somebody to come and get me.' That made it worse when I would ask people where I was.

"Eventually, by my third trip back to the hotel, they realized I was pretty desperate. I was getting real serious, like, 'I'll pay you. I'll give you a credit card number over the phone. You can charge me a room. Do whatever you have to do.'

"They let me call, and I got in touch with our manager—he's been our manager forever, so I knew his number. I called him…and, of course, he didn't answer because it's LA. He's not up. I was like, 'Son of a bitch.'

"They dialed the number again for me, and eventually he answers.

"I was like, 'Gary. They left me at a truck stop, and I don't know where we are or where we're going to go.'

"He was waking up—'What?'

"I said, 'Just call Joe, our tour manager, and tell him they left me at a truck stop.'

"He does his thing, and he calls me back and [says], 'Dude, you're like a hundred miles away from the gig…The bus driver is sleeping. They got to sleep because they drive through the night.'

"He's really bummed out. So he's like, 'I gotta work

this out. You're a hundred miles away. I got to try and get you a ride.'

"So eventually he gets me a cab that we pay through the teeth for to take me to the [gig]. We paid like hundreds of dollars for that ride. I get there, and the kick-in-the-balls part was everybody was looking at me like, 'Hey, what's up?'…Everybody is just acting normal. I was like, 'Don't you guys know what happened to me?'

"They were like, 'No. Did you just wake up?'"

—*DENNIS CASEY*, FLOGGING MOLLY

DROWNING POOL

Despite running through singers the way Spinal Tap did drummers, Drowning Pool continues to be one of the most consistent forces in the alt-metal scene. The Dallas quartet was launched in 1996 by guitarist C. J. Pierce, bassist Stevie Benton and drummer Mike Luce, and by the ensuing decade had secured frequent slots on the festival circuit, from Ozzfest to WrestleMania.

"It was on a Sunday night in Salt Lake City, Utah. Friday and Saturday nights had been spent playing LA and Vegas. Not only did we play those cities, we took full advantage of the excess both cities offered. We pulled into Salt Lake on Sunday, sleep deprived and very hung over…Everything came apart during the show—speakers blew, guitars went out of tune. Our enthusiasm was gone by the end of the third song. Toward the end of the set, however, most of the crowd had come to life even though we were barely hanging on. Prior to the last song, Dave [Williams, former singer] had the audience fired up.

"'Give it up for heavy metal!' he screamed.

"The crowd roared back!

"'Give it up for alcohol!'

"The crowd roared louder! Dave had them right where he wanted them.

"With his final anthem, he cried, 'Give it up for Satan!'

"Not a peep from the crowd. It was one of those classic moments when you hear crickets chirp. We played the last song and walked off the stage in silence."

—STEVIE BENTON, DROWNING POOL

JOHN SCOFIELD

With dozens of acclaimed albums to his credit and numerous high-profile collaborations, fusion luminary John Scofield has joined the likes of Pat Metheny and Bill Frisell as one of the most respected guitarists in modern jazz. The Ohio native and Berklee College of Music alum made a name thanks to his nimble fingers and a distinctive, distorted guitar tone that is more muted than piercing. From 1982 to 1985, the guitarist scored his most significant assignment, recording and touring with pioneering jazz trumpeter Miles Davis. Scofield embarked on a solo career thereafter, often collaborating with acts not initially associated with jazz rock, such as John Mayer, Gov't Mule and Medeski, Martin & Wood.

"I've played amazingly hilarious gigs in my life, back before I was known as a guitarist—when I was just jobbin' around, as they say…I was a music student in 1970 in Boston. Me and my friend Dave Samuels [of Spyro Gyra], a vibraphonist who is pretty well known in jazz [circles], we were both Berklee students at Berklee College of Music. We got a call to play a St. Patrick's Day gig in Chelsea, Massachusetts—which is an Irish town right outside of Boston—with some Irish drummer we didn't know. So we're just supposed to show up there.

"We showed up and set up our instruments, and the guy set up his drums, and he was the lead singer, too. So this is a weird instrumentation to begin with: vibes, guitar and a [drummer-singer]. And this guy was Irish, as in from Dublin.

"We're in some Sons of Ireland…hall in this real working-class place. So we pick up our instruments and people come in, and he says, [in accent] 'Let's start with "Mrs. O'Flannery's Cow."'"

"And we said, 'Well, we don't know that one.'

"Then he starts to run this list of traditional Irish tunes, and we had no idea what he was talking about, of course. So he said, 'Just FOLLOW ME.'

"So he starts to play the drums and sing. And we had no idea what to do. So we started to just play little chords and try to follow what key he was in. And we were fucking up. He's singing, 'And Mrs. Flannery went to town / And then came back in the mornin'.' And he's looking at us, and the audience is starting to look at us like, 'What the fuck? Everybody knows "Mrs. Flannery's Cow."'"

"He went from one tune to another. Then the audience started to boo us. He was getting real mad and said, 'Come on. Play with me. Play with me.'

"The audience is drunk—they'd been drinking all day. So finally, this little eighty-year-old guy says, 'Get the fuck off the stage.' And he pulls out this upright piano and starts to play with the drummer. So we just started to slink in the background, standing there with our instruments as this guy began to take over. Then we just sort of unplugged to go get in the car and leave.

"I can't believe that it happened, but it did."

—JOHN SCOFIELD

BERNARD PURDIE

Bernard Purdie is known as the world's most recorded drummer. He has played on thousands of songs, collaborating with artists such as James Brown, Aretha Franklin, Miles Davis, Steely Dan, Bette Midler and Bob Marley. The Maryland native is also known for inventing the Purdie Shuffle. His intricate signature groove turns up on a number of artists' tracks—Steely Dan's "Babylon Sisters," for instance. And, yes, that's him behind the drum kit on iconic tracks such as "The Hustle" and "The Theme from Shaft."

"Not too many people have ever asked me that. I can't call it the worst, but I'll tell you the one I tried to mess up because I was angry. They asked me to play like I was a fourteen-year-old. I was upset. Here I am, the number-one drummer in New York and around the country, and they want me to sound like a fourteen-year-old. So I tried to mess up the song. That song has haunted me for [forty-five] years: 'Hang on Sloopy.'

"They wanted me to sound like a beginner. They wanted me to sound like a trash band, a garage band. They didn't use those terms then…What made it even worse is that the producer and a couple of the guys in the band had been smokin' and drinkin'. It made me very, very upset. So I tried putting fills in every place but where I was supposed to. Once I've told the story around, then people listen to the song differently and say, 'Oh, yeah, you would normally never put a fill here and not do this here.'

"That's what happened. But I was trying to mess it up. And when we finished, they were like, 'That's it! That's perfect! That's the one!'

"I said to myself then, that as long you live, if you don't like something or don't want to do it with somebody, then don't take the job. You cannot go with the wrong attitude to do a job when somebody is paying you. If you don't want to do the job, don't accept the job. So that has been my motto."

—BERNARD PURDIE

TREASURE FINGERS

CREDIT: RYAN PURCELL

Producer-DJ Ashley Jones spent a decade on the international club circuit with the drum-and-bass group Evol Intent. He recently deployed as a solo act under the name Treasure Fingers, administering nimble remixes and originals that stress punchy synth hooks and mobile bass lines. The Atlanta-based artist is best known for "Cross the Dancefloor," a vocoder-driven track that became a club anthem and spawned dozens of remixes.

◆ ◆ ◆

"I got a new worst gig—I used to have another one—but I've got a new one as of this past January [2011]. I was in Australia, and it was billed as a beach party. It was on Australia Day, which is kind of like their Fourth of July. So I show up, and it's in a warehouse, inside, like 3 or 4 p.m., there's no beach in sight—[not] even outside. It would be the equivalent of, like, if someone decided to throw a party in a club in the afternoon on Fourth of July when everyone was off and having parties at the beach or whatever. It's pretty sparse, and the room that I was on, the guys before me actually decided to stop.

"They're like, 'We're done with this.'

"They left. So there's no music playing in there. So they come and grab me to go start playing. I walk in there, and the guys had switched the flat-screen [TV] on the walls…to show a cricket game. There are like three or four or five guys just sitting in the middle of the dance floor watching this flat-screen cricket game.

"The promoter is like, 'You've got to go on. You've got to bring this back to life.'

"I was like, 'This is gonna be impossible.'

"I literally just turned it on and put on a CD really quiet, apologized to the cricket fans and let the CD play for an hour, looping over and over."

—*ASHLEY JONES,* TREASURE FINGERS

MOBY GRAPE

Taking its quirky name from the punch line of the joke, "What's big and purple and lives in the ocean?" Moby Grape became one of the primary movers and shakers in the Bay Area music scene of the late 1960s. Critics consider the band a standout of the era for its lively mingling of folk, blues, country and psychedelic sounds. Founder Jerry Miller was recently ranked sixty-eighth in **Rolling Stone's** list "Top 100 Greatest Guitarists of All Time," placing him ahead of such heavyweights as Eddie Van Halen, Pink Floyd's David Gilmour and AC/DC's Angus Young.

"We did one at the Fillmore East where we sat down. [Promoter] Bill Graham had a fit. He said, 'All you guys needed was coffins.' But some of the new generation thought it was really alternative. They just shit a brick. They thought we were the coolest thing ever. Yet we didn't understand what we were really obligated to do, which was to come on and give people what they wanted: 'Omaha' ass kicking like it should have been. That was a valuable lesson…The audience was the cream of the crop (in the Bay Area scene of the '60s)—not so much the musicians. It was the blessing of the audience. They gave and gave. The Grateful Dead and Big Brother and Jefferson Airplane were oftentimes very sour—and Moby Grape was from time to time very sour. We had no tuners and (the PA systems) weren't great. But the audience was right there with you, always."

—JERRY MILLER, MOBY GRAPE

NEW DUNCAN IMPERIALS

CREDIT: JAY LEE

Pigtail Dick (guitar and vocals), Skipper Zwackinov (bass, balloons and vocal) and Goodtime Dammit (drums, drums, drums) started New Duncan Imperials in 1989 for a laugh, honing a campy brand of rock in the basement of Dick's mother's house. Soon they were named the best live band in the city by both the **Chicago Reader** *and* **Chicago Tribune.**

◆ ◆ ◆

"We did this show in Finland at a cultural center in Helsinki. They set us up in like an art gallery. It was really echoey, and we were all jet-lagged because it was right after we got there. It was so awful. They didn't like us. We didn't know how to charm them because we didn't know how to speak Finnish—I don't think anyone speaks Finnish outside of Finland. Then we were so loud that we knocked this art off the wall. It involved these half eggshells glued into it. It ruined the work of art, and they wanted us to pay for it…something in kronas. It was way more than we were getting."

–PIGTAIL DICK, NEW DUNCAN IMPERIALS

BILL LYNCH

The R&B guitarist-singer Bill Lynch has shared the stage with performers such as Jerry Lee Lewis, Bonnie Raitt, Bo Diddley, Stevie Ray Vaughan and Bruce Willis, but he's probably best known for his long-time collaborations with keyboard icon Mike Finnigan. He is also fondly remembered as the singer of the theme to the Emmy-nominated It's Garry Shandling's Show (1986–1990). Who could forget the catchy ditty: "This is the theme to Garry's Show. / The opening theme to Garry's show. / This is the music that you hear as you watch the credits." Lynch currently fronts an all-star band called the Midwestern Icons.

"**H**armonica player Juke Logan and I were hired to open up and play with Homesick James. He claimed to have written 'Shake Your Moneymaker.' The guy was in his eighties and so obstinate. He hated us because we were white. He refused to tune.

"When we walked out onstage I said, 'I have a tuner if you want it.' He took total offense. He said, 'Boy, I've got A440 ears. Don't touch my guitar.'

"So Juke and I get out there and play half a dozen songs. Then it was time for Homesick James. This was at the Music Machine, and the place was absolutely packed with blues fans coming out to see this living legend. The three of us were sitting on the stage in chairs, and Homesick James was sitting between me and Juke. The whole time he was stirring up trouble. He'd lean over and say something to me, then mutter something to Juke. The whole thing was just horrible.

"I took a walk between shows just to cool down. I didn't know if I wanted to go back in and play with this guy. But the show must go on. So I got back onstage with him, and the second set he was even more out of tune. It was horrendous. I had resorted to just making rhythmic noises. He'd lean over and say, 'Play.' He would change chords whenever he felt like it.

"So he blows in an ending out of the blue, and Juke missed it and played an extra note. James snickered and leaned in to me and said, 'Never send a boy to do a man's job.'

"With this, I figured, 'I am done!'

"So I grabbed the microphone and said, 'Ladies and gentlemen, Homesick James!'

"He appeared sort of disoriented because it seemed weird that I all of a sudden turned into some kind of announcer.

"I said, 'Can you believe it? Right here on our stage, a living legend: Homesick James!'

"He was just staring at me. The crowd was kind of stirring.

"Then I said, 'I can't believe I'm sitting next to Homesick James!'

"Then I said his name over and over until he stood up, threw his guitar down and left the stage.

"They wrote a review of the show in a local blues publication. In the review I remember one line that I loved. It said, 'The second set was wrought with malice.'"

—BILL LYNCH

KINKY FRIEDMAN

Kinky Friedman's career pursuits include songwriter, novelist, humorist, cigar entrepreneur and onetime Texas gubernatorial candidate. Born Richard S. Friedman, he was given his nickname, due to his kinky hair, by songwriter Chinga Chavin. In the early 1970s his band Kinky Friedman and the Texas Jewboys found a unique niche in pop culture as a satirical country-western act. Songs "The Ballad of Charles Whitman," "They Ain't Making Jews Like Jesus Anymore" and "Get Your Biscuits in the Oven and Your Buns in Bed" turned into cult classics, impressing heavyweights such as Bob Dylan, who often joined Friedman on tour.

"Saturday Night Live was a disaster [in 1976]. That was a great opportunity. I should have fit right in. We had a great version of 'Charles Whitman' ready to roll. We'd already rehearsed with John [Belushi], Danny Aykroyd and Steve Martin—'the sniper in the tower'—it was hilarious. And they canned it just before I went on, and that put me in a petulant snit. I got really wrongways with all the producers and stuff. They had a legal problem with the family of Charles Whitman, so they caved in right at the end. But that would have been perfect. It would have been killer. It was a major production number. But right at the last minute I was left just doing this ballad by myself—'Dear Abbie' about Abbie Hoffman—and that was kind of weak…But there have been a lot of worst shows, because I'm not really a musician. It's the curse of being multi-talented. No one takes you seriously. And the people who love my books and take them seriously don't even know I write music—and vice versa. If I could have gotten those audiences together, but now it's too late. I'm in my sixties, which is too young for Medicare and too old for women to care."

—KINKY FRIEDMAN

R/D

San Francisco's R. D. White—who goes by the stage name R/D—represents a new generation of artists crafting original electronic dance music that weaves indie rock into the mix. Although best known for his studio remixes of other artists, R/D expertly incorporates live instruments into his dynamic DJ sets.

"**M**y worst story takes place in Los Angeles at the Viper Room, which was made famous by River Phoenix dying there. We had booked the show with Andrea Parker, who was a really big female DJ back when Warped Records was predominantly electronic—they had Aphex Twin and Plaid.

"The bouncers at the door were being unbelievable. Basically, just giving her the worst time. She's—I don't want to say cocky—but she can get pretty ghetto. She starts cussing them out, and I'm trying to calm her down so she doesn't fuck things up. My girlfriend at the time was really fiery. She was like the same way, just constantly going at this bouncer. Finally, they get in.

"[My girlfriend] starts taking pictures. Well, you can't take pictures in the club because 'it's a place where famous people go.' She keeps taking pictures.

"The bouncer is like, 'One more time and you're out of here.'

"So we have this tension all night long with the bouncer, the lead bartender—all of them hate us.

"It's 1 a.m. and it's pretty thin. It wasn't a very good turnout. I had already played. And the stage manager closes an electric curtain on Andrea Parker… while she's playing. Here's our headline act that we had brought from the United Kingdom. She is fucking pissed.

"I tell my girlfriend, 'Let's just go break down and get the fuck out of here.'

"Andrea has this drink—this cocktail—up on the mixer. She spills a little bit on the mixer by accident. Then she looks back and is like, 'Fuck it!'

"We both get in this mode of like, 'Fuck this place.'

"The stage manager parts the curtain and comes up onstage. He looks at his mixer and is like, 'What the fuck is this?'

"He starts freaking out: 'This is my mixer. You guys

did this…We got cameras back there. I'm gonna check the cameras out.'

"We pack everything up and decide to get out of there.

"I jump down, get all my gear and my girlfriend takes off with Andrea Parker in another car. I'm going around the corner, and this one bouncer—I don't know why he wanted to do this—he pulls me aside and says, 'Hey, bro, I just wanted to say how sorry I am. Things went down really whack.'

"I'm like, 'Yeah, yeah, it's cool.'

"I keep trying to get away. Finally, I break away from him and jump in my car. I have the choice to go right or left. And I make the wrong choice. I turn left. I go up to the top of the street, and the cops pull up.

"They're like, 'Get out of the car,' with their flashlights.

"Then the stage manager tech, the lead bartender, the bartender and the door guy are all standing there like, 'Oh, you're fucked, bro.'

"I don't know what to do. [The cops] throw me in handcuffs, throw me in the back of the cop car, and they're like, 'We have you on video vandalizing equipment inside.'

"The cop is like, 'You need to pay restitution or you're going to jail.'

"[I tell him,] 'My girlfriend took all the door money. I don't have any cash. I will give you all the cash for whatever that mixer is worth. Just don't put me in jail.'

"So he pulls out my phone, scrolls down and dials my ex-girlfriend's number. 'Hello, is this so-and-so?'

"She's like, 'Who is this?'—she's still all fiery.

"'This is the Los Angeles Police Department. I have your boyfriend in the back of my police car, unless you pay X amount of dollars for this mixer that you ruined...'

"She just starts freaking out.

"'Put him on the phone. This is bullshit!'

"[The cop] looks at me with this weird look, and he holds the phone up because I'm still cuffed.

"I'm like, 'Babe?'

"'I can't fuckin' believe you got caught. Why didn't you just get the fuck out of there?'

"She was blaming me for not running fast enough, and I was like, 'I'm in the back of a police car, about to go to jail. Maybe you want to come?'

"'Fuck that. I'm not blah, blah, blah.'

"The guy pulls the phone away, and I'm like, 'She hung up.'

"He's like, 'Are you sure that she's your girlfriend?'

"I have the brilliant idea as I'm sitting there: 'I will go to an ATM machine that's close by. You can escort me there, and we'll get the total amount.'

"So he uncuffs me, marches me into this liquor store, and I get the maximum amount...He's gonna hold the money and the mixer, then he wants me to go to Guitar Center. It was a whole three-day thing.

"The cherry on top is that is the last straw for me and my girlfriend. I was with her for seven years. We lived together and everything."

—R/D

STEVE LUKATHER

CREDIT: ROB SHANAHAN

One of the all-time great session guitarists, Steve Lukather is also a founding member of the band Toto, best known for top-five hits such as "Africa," "Hold the Line" and "Rosanna." In addition to winning five Grammy Awards and selling thirty-five million albums with Toto, Lukather's blistering guitar work appears on more than 1,500 records, including staple hits such as Michael Jackson's "Beat It," Don Henley's "Dirty Laundry" and Olivia Newton-John's "Physical"—which was the number-one single of the 1980s.

◆ ◆ ◆

"I started doing A-level sessions when I was about nineteen years old. Toto was starting, and I had just come out of Boz Scaggs' band. I began to get all these calls for really cool records. For years I was doing twenty-five sessions a week, plus the band. I worked my way up to the top of the food chain as a session guitar player.

"I would get these calls, 'We need you for a week at Capitol Studios, twelve to six.'

"You didn't ask too many questions. You often didn't know who the artist was. It could be Aretha Franklin or Barbra Streisand or whomever. It was just fun to do. Am I going to sit around the house and not work? When people give me a call, I'm going to go play. For years I took everything that came my way and didn't ask too many questions. I didn't care because I loved the challenge of doing different kinds of music.

"Well, there was one day I realized, 'This is the end of me taking every call and not asking who it is.'

"I get a call from a guy who says, 'I need you at Sunset Sound from twelve to six, Monday through Friday.'

"I show up and there are three rooms going on. I walk into the main studio and I realize the 'artist' is Richard Simmons, the health guru.

"First off, what the fuck is a Richard Simmons record?

"Apparently, it is a 'dancercise' record. And the music is fucking awful.

"I have a guitar tech with me at the time who'd just had a bunch of teeth pulled out. He has a fistful of Vicodins and is lying on the couch. I'm looking around, thinking, 'This is awful. But I've got to be professional here.'

"I'm running through the music, and they're these horrible disco-era tunes. Music for rotund people to lose weight to. Richard Simmons is there in his little striped shorts. It's like we're doing a cheap TV show or something. I'm mortified by all this.

"At the studio, there's this courtyard in the middle where everybody meets to play basketball and stuff—you can hang out with the other musicians and producers. Everyone is like, 'Who are you working with today?'

"I'm like, 'It's Richard (mumble, mumble).'

"They start laughing at me. This is not the reputation I have or need. So I figure I got to get out of this shit somehow.

"I go back in, and Richard Simmons comes out to where my tech is asleep on the couch, all drugged up from the pain. Richard Simmons starts kissing him. This is a guy who looks like he's a hardened criminal; we're not talking about a pretty boy. He wakes up and is like, 'What the fuck, man?'

"I figure, 'I got to get out of here!'

"So I say, 'Excuse me, I need to use the phone.' This is pre–cell phone in the early 1980s. But instead of using the phone, I go out to my car and leave. I never call back. I never go back in. This is the first time I have ever walked on a session. As a professional musician, my reputation is to be a pro, show up on time, have my shit together. I'd done a couple cheesy sessions, but this is beyond cheese. This is putting my ass through the glory hole.

"I thought, 'That's it. I'm done. I'm never doing a session again unless I know who it is and I like the music.'

"So I get a call a few days later for another session at Sunset Sound. I show up, and they're all still there: the producer and Richard Simmons. But I don't know this. I'm working on a session with [Toto drummer] Jeff Porcaro in another room. [Simmons's] producer finds out I'm in the building, and he comes over and wants to fight me.

"He is chewing me out. 'Motherfucker, how dare you…'

"I'm like, 'The music was shit. Sorry. What do you want me to do?'

"This guy starts coming at me.

"Lenny Castro, the famous percussionist and one of my oldest pals, is also there. He's from New York—a Puerto Rican badass. He has a knife belt; the actual buckle of his belt is a knife. This guy comes at me, and Lenny pushes me aside and takes his belt off and suddenly has a knife in his hand. He's like, 'Are you ready? Are you really gonna come at my boy?'

"There is a whole scuffle with people all over the place. It's a big, ugly scene. Nobody draws any blood. But it's a little heated for a moment.

"After that, I swore I would never ever again whore myself out being a musician."

—STEVE LUKATHER

Dan Wilson is responsible for penning major hits on two contemporary classics that took Album of the Year honors at the Grammy Awards: Adele's "21" in 2012 and Dixie Chicks' "Taking the Long Way" in 2007. But it was with his own band, Semisonic, that Wilson created one of the 1990s most durable tunes. His "Closing Time" is an alt-rock smash still seemingly omnipresent in TV shows, movies and sporting event PAs. The songwriter decided to approach a worst gig saga through the help of a conference call with his fellow Minneapolis bandmates.

SEMISONIC'S WORST SHOWS EVER:
A CONFERENCE CALL

By Dan Wilson

CREDIT: EMERLEE SHERMAN

When I was first asked to write about my "worst gig ever," I knew I might have a little trouble doing it. First of all, I've played upward of 2,000 gigs in my life, between college bands, Trip Shakespeare, Semisonic, my solo shows and guesting on other people's concerts. There are a lot of shows to choose from.

Secondly, one thing about my memory of gigs is that everything about them sticks out in my mind—except for the shows themselves. The dressing rooms, the parking areas, the fans hanging out near the bus—I can remember those atmospheric details. But there are only a few performances that I can actually picture in my mind.

Third, I have a rose-colored-glasses issue. I'm sure I've endured a lot of bad experiences, but somehow they magically fade into the mists of time, and I'm left remembering the good stuff.

So I decided to get my Semisonic bandmates, bassist John Munson and drummer Jacob Slichter, on the phone. Jacob (we call him Jake) is the author of a widely read memoir of his days in Semisonic, *So You Wanna Be a Rock and Roll Star?* It's a really funny book, and at times it reads like a greatest-hits collection of worst-ever gigs. And John, like Jake, has a better memory than I do, as well as an easily stirred sense of outrage, which I knew would be helpful when describing horrible gigs.

FALLING OFF THE STAGE

Dan: Wasn't there a time or two that I fell off the stage?

Jake: You fell off the stage once in Cleveland, I think.

Dan: And once in Madison, Wisconsin?

John: Was it in Cleveland? I think it might have also happened in Kansas City, maybe at that bar in Westport...

Dan and Jake: The Hurricane?

John: At the Hurricane also...

Dan: But I decided that doesn't really count as worst gig ever, these isolated moments of tumbling off a stage.

John: No, but definitely it's gotta be among the...it's embarrassing. I was embarrassed!

Jake: I have several nominees. There was the "Semisonic Must Suck" show in Kansas City, which is a certain kind of worst gig ever, intentionally so.

SEMISONIC MUST SUCK

Elektra, our record label at the time of the "Semisonic Must Suck" show, was considering whether to keep us on their roster, and we wanted off, partly because Elektra had been sitting on our recently finished album. Rival label MCA had indicated they would sign us to a new deal if Elektra dropped us. So Elektra sent an A&R guy to a show in Kansas City to see if we were worth keeping, and our mission was to bore him into dropping us from the label. It worked, the A&R guy was bored, Elektra dropped us and we got picked up by MCA shortly afterwards. A sordid tale all around.

Jake: The worst part was trying to wrap our heads around how we could go up on stage and actually...

Dan: ...try to be bad...

Jake: ...since, you know, we were being asked to override the hardwired mission of every musician in the name of getting free of our record contract. So there was that gig. And then there was the "giant beer bottle" show.

THE GIANT BEER BOTTLE SHOW

At a show at Irving Plaza in New York City, we learned that our label, MCA, and the sponsor, Guinness, had arranged for us to dance with a man in a giant beer bottle costume during the song "Closing Time." When we were told about this just minutes before our set, I said, "No way! I'm not going to dance with no giant beer bottle." This led to a very tense and escalating sequence of bargaining and threats, somehow culminating with the radio station WPLJ in New York telling us that if we didn't dance with the beer bottle, the station wouldn't play our singles. And MCA told us that if WPLJ stopped playing our singles, other stations would follow, and we would never have a hit again. I replied that if they sent the guy in the beer bottle outfit onto our stage, we would roll him back off into the wings. We did the gig, without the beer bottle guy, and I believe WPLJ did in fact stop playing our songs.

Dan: The message was that if you don't do what you're told, you're not gonna get played on the radio anymore and it's the beginning of the end or something. There were a lot of threats floating around before the beginning of that show.

John: God, it's like you had to not give a rip about anything, but at the same time you had to give a rip...ugh, it was horrible.

Dan: The interesting thing is that even though it qualifies as the worst backstage moment of any show ever, I don't remember anything about the show itself, but I imagine we played pretty well.

Jake: The show was a good one!

Dan: But it was the worst politics surrounding any show ever.

Jake: Right.

John: OK, for me, Fuji Rock was also epically, horribly bad...

THE FUJI ROCK FESTIVAL

John: The Mt. Fuji Rock Festival in Japan...that was fucking brutal. Oh my God, that was horrid. That was a fucking nightmare.

Dan: OK, I remember....I had lost my voice and couldn't sing a note above a D, so you guys had to sing all the choruses for me.

Jake: Yeah, we had to sing the choruses, and I just hated it.

Dan: It was too bad I couldn't sing.

John: That was bad.

Jake: And then we had to go and watch Oasis hold the crowd spellbound afterward. That was torture.

Dan: But it might not have been so bad from the audience's perspective.

Jake: Or from a storytelling perspective—I mean, it would probably get my vote for worst gig, but it's maybe not the best story of a worst gig because basically the story is that Dan had blown out his voice and we had to do the singing.

John: It was that, yeah, but the lead up to it is somewhat interesting. It seems to me a lot of these supposed worst gigs happened very late in the game, when the stakes were something different than what we were gunning for earlier in our career. In the beginning we were trying to heroically win for ourselves. But then later, all of a sudden we were trying to win for other people. That's when things got weird for me. I don't mind failing if the stakes are, "I failed you guys and I failed myself." But it starts to get really uncomfortable and weird when it's, "I'm failing our manager" or "I'm failing the record company, and…"

Dan: "…the radio station."

ICONS AND LABYRINTHS

Jake: Right, then there's the Billboard Awards show. Let me make a case for the Billboard Awards being the worst gig ever, because…

John: You've already written this story, though, right? It's in your book.

Jake: Okay, I have, I have. I'm happy to disqualify it purely on that basis alone.

Dan: Wait a minute, wait a second, hold on! We can

recycle from Jake's book. If you can only tell your good stories one time in life, you're in for a hard life.

Jake: Let me tell you why it's great: because everything right up until the ending is awesome. We get there, we're interviewed by the media, we're backstage mingling with our musical heroes and various pop stars, we graciously pass up our rehearsal slot, we take the 23-yard limousine ride around the corner to the front of the building, we get out, we walk down the red carpet and get screamed at by excited fans, we're processing the sudden hugeness of our profile that has sort of surprised us.

Dan: Jake, Jake, why did we give up our rehearsal slot?

Jake: Because they were all running late, all of the production. Everybody was taking too much time, all of the big stars whom we were soon to mingle with and count ourselves lucky to be among—you know, the Mariah Careys...

Dan: (Laughing) Cher, Garth Brooks...

Jake: Courtney Love...

John: Right, and being interviewed with Natalie Imbruglia and getting to look at her and think, "Wow, she's cute..."

Dan: Wasn't the backstage setup like a cluster of mobile homes underneath a highway or something?

Jake: No, it was sort of like a locker room or big labyrinth. In fact, our guide got lost! It was so labyrinth-themed that on numerous occasions the woman who had been assigned to get us from our dressing room to the stage or to our seats didn't know where the fuck she was going, and we followed her to various dead-ends so we had to keep turning around and going back to where we started.

THE BILLBOARD AWARDS ADVENTURE

Semisonic went to Las Vegas in December of 1998 to perform our song "Closing Time" on the Billboard Awards. The awards show was held at the MGM Grand Hotel. For the performers, it was a three-day event. We all arrived on Saturday early in the day. Our crew quickly went to work gambling and drinking. Jake stayed in his room to read a book. John disappeared to play roulette with the band Hole. I went to an art exhibit in one of the casinos. In the hotel lobby and its environs we saw dozens of pop stars and musicians whose albums we had either admired or ridiculed. Later in the day there was a rehearsal and technical run-through. We were going to need it because for that particular show, my singing would be live but the band's instrumental performance would be mimed to a playback of the instrumental mix of the song.

Jake: I remember that Saturday when we arrived I saw The Sugar Hill Gang, and I went up to Hank from that group and said, "Hey, I just want to say when 'Rapper's Delight' came out I was just instantly hooked." And before I could get to my second sentence he said, "Which way to the food?" And the day ended on a similar note, because I said to Jay-Z, at a party where there was loud music playing, "I really enjoyed 'Hard Knock Life,'" and he exhaled from a cigar and spoke in such a low frequency that I couldn't understand a word he said, and I just nodded politely and let him alone.

John: Then at the show itself, the performers were all in a kind of holding area together backstage, so we were waiting with Cher and Courtney Love.

Dan: Stevie Wonder was standing around backstage.

Jake: Magic Johnson sat near us during the performance. Musicians were coming up to him to pay him tribute.

John: It was the most shoulder-rubbing celebrity thing I think we ever did. Maybe the Grammys were a little more…maybe I was closer to a few more of my heroes at the Grammys than I was at the Billboard Awards, but the Billboard Awards was surprisingly well-stocked.

Dan: Wasn't there something about Garth Brooks flying through the air?

Jake: He did, during the show. Well, we saw him run in backstage to get made up so he could run out to the front of the auditorium to make his entrance from the sky. From above. You know, from the catwalks or whatever. Anyway, we're backstage and Garth Brooks storms into the dressing room in a rush because he's gotta get to his zip-line to make his flying entrance onto the stage and we're eagerly watching. We'd been such good sports to skip our sound-check, and all the crew was so appreciative of how we gave up our rehearsal time and allowed ourselves to get pushed back further and further in the show. I remember walking by Whitney Houston and her background vocalists as they were singing and snapping their fingers in the hallway rehearsing their harmonies, and I was like, "I can't fucking believe I am walking by Whitney Houston singing a cappella." Their singing was mind blowing.

John: Yeah, they did sound awesome. Whitney in particular was really sweating.

Dan: A lot.

Jake: We had been outfitted with special suits.

John: Quite sharp, tight-fitting English-cut suits.

Jake: That was part of the whole Cloud Nine thing before the gig...before the cold chute-ride to the bottom. So, Hole goes on right before us and then it's the end of the show and our big moment and we're thinking about performing for Stevie Wonder, Carole King, Jay-Z. And the production people are nervously looking at their watches, in a panic about running over the network time limit.

A RACE AGAINST "TIME"

The conceit was that Semisonic would come on at the end of the Awards show and play "Closing Time." The song would "close" the show. But due to the structure of these events, the last performance in the show is 1) the least likely to get a proper rehearsal, and 2) the most likely to be cut short if the rest of the show runs long. So, unbeknownst to the band, there was some concern among our label and management that the band might not even get a chance to perform. Nobody told us because they knew it would enrage us and possibly cause us to telekinetically trigger earthquakes and tidal waves in distant countries.

John: And the union, any time you're doing a union show... you know the union guys. The show had already gone over so much that they're at time-and-a-half, and if they go to double-time then the producer makes no money.

Jake: Yeah, and there was a guy in a truck, because Jim (our manager) and Jay (the president of our label) were back-stage, in contact with the truck, and the guy in a truck basically had his hand on the power lever because union hours have now gone into quintuple overtime and the production guy has got his ear on that. So as soon as the network cut the live show's signal, the lever came down, and with the lever the pants came down....So we got out onstage at the end of the awards show. Dan starts singing and then John and I are just waiting to come in, and we come in, we hit the first chorus, we're rocking along, I'm about to play the drum fill into the second verse and just as we get there...the power to the stage goes off, our mics are cut, the house lights go on and a voice says, "Thank you for coming to the 1999 Billboard Awards!" And we're left standing...

Dan: ...cut off halfway through the song, with no warning.

John: You know, we're depantsed.

Jake: We're completely depantsed in front of Stevie Wonder, Carole King, the whole audience at the MGM Grand Arena.

John: Whenever anybody asks me what the exact sensation of that moment was, I'm like, think about being out in front of your gym class and the girl you have a crush on is there and all of your friends are there and then the creepy stinker from your class creeps up behind you and pulls your pants down thinking that you have on a jockstrap but you forgot your underwear and you're just there swinging in the wind in front of everyone. It's just a classic depantsed moment where, maybe they didn't even intend for you to be fully naked, but you were fully naked.

Dan: The thing about the Billboard Awards is that we were actually sort of rocking. Or I was singing and you guys were pretending to rock and I was half pretending to rock, but you know, it was a big crowd of people and it seemed to be going really well and it was dark—the audience is dark and there are lights on us. It was very production-y and then suddenly, halfway through the song, very instantaneously the sound from the stage stops, and the house lights come on, and we're standing there awkwardly in silence in front of the crowd.

Jake: Right. It was over in a flash.

Dan: It was crushing!

John: I mean, we literally got through one chorus and that was it. The producers really just wanted to hear that one line because it was "closing time" and that would wrap up the show.

Jake: Perhaps the coda to the story is when we showed up to play the Penn and Teller show six weeks later, also in Vegas, and some of the same crew members saw us. They came up to Dan and said, "We're so sorry about what happened to you guys and we're gonna bend over backward to make sure everything goes well tonight." And Dan said, "Yeah, after we bent forward last time!"

GARBAGE

Devised in 1994 by Scottish ingenue Shirley Manson and veteran record producers Butch Vig, Steve Marker and Duke Erikson, Garbage surfed the decade's alternative wave with hits such as "Only Happy When It Rains," "Stupid Girl" and "#1 Crush." Before long, the group's studio wizardry, songwriting skills and charismatic waifish singer made it an MTV mainstay and multi-Platinum seller.

◆ ◆ ◆

"**T**wo stick in my head. Part of it is because of the extremes of the gig. One, we did a radio show on the first tour called Snoasis, which was in upstate New York at a ski lodge in front of twenty thousand kids. It was this outdoor festival and all the kids were in parkas. Oasis was supposed to be the headliner—there were ten bands each doing a half-hour set—and they canceled when Noel Gallagher said, 'Fuck it. I'm not going to sing in twenty-below weather.'

"It was absolutely freezing out. They said, 'You guys have to go on and play a longer set.'

"So we went on, and we couldn't keep the guitar strings in tune. I was wearing a parka and gloves—you can't really play drums in that. Shirley had a complete face mask. It could have been anybody singing. You wouldn't even know it was her until you heard her voice. It sounded so bad that after two or three songs the kids were getting impatient because they wanted to rock out and we kept stopping and changing guitars. Finally, we just played a couple punk covers, and after fifteen minutes onstage we bailed. Then the kids started throwing snowballs. It was an absolute disaster.

"The other extreme is we played the Fuji Fest in 1998 right before Korn, in front of thirty thousand kids who were moshing like crazy. But the Japanese mosh more politely, so it was a different vibe. But it was so fucking hot. It was 110 degrees out and 95 percent humidity. It was just sweltering.

"We went onstage and we're playing with a pretty intense *c'est la vie [joie de vivre]*, and about halfway through the second song we were all crushed by heat-stroke. Shirley had to sit on the front of the stage. There was no escape from the sun. It was like three or four in the afternoon, and the sun was right in our face. There was nowhere to hide from it. I remember one of the crew guys brought out an umbrella to hold over her. I was having water poured over me between every song. We made it through an hour set, but we were all beet red. I thought Steve—who was still valiantly trying to thrash on the guitar—was going to have to be hospitalized. He looked like a lobster. Shirley was sunburned. Even though she put on sunscreen, it just melts and goes in your eyes.

"Physically, it was a terrible show. We're not a band that likes the sun. If you're a Blink-182 from California, you can go onstage and jump around in your boxer shorts. But we're from Wisconsin and Scotland. We like mood lighting. We need all the mood lighting we can get."

—*BUTCH VIG*, GARBAGE

CONCRETE BLONDE

A three-piece band that never got pigeonholed into one style, Concrete Blonde was one of the rare harder-rock groups in the late 1980s and early 1990s to be fronted by a female singer. Johnette Napolitano's undeniable voice—gritty, passionate, honest to a fault—made quite an impression on the legion of fans that remember Concrete Blonde as among the best of the college-rock acts to precede the alternative boom. Taking shape as Dream 6, Napolitano and guitarist James Mankey kicked around the LA club scene for five years before landing a contract with IRS Records. While its self-titled debut yielded the punky MTV hit "Still in Hollywood," Concrete Blonde didn't crack the top twenty until its 1990 album Bloodletting yielded the plaintive anthem "Joey."

"Chicago, and it was years ago. It was 116 degrees, and we had to drive in our RV from New Mexico to Chicago. Chicago has always been a good town for us…and the show was sold out. We had a crew that was—let's say—'substandard'…It was so hot—and I had my cat on the road with me—that I had to put my cat in the refrigerator in the RV. We blew a couple tires, and it was hell getting tires on the RV because it's an odd size, and it's Sunday or whatever. And the crew kept going, 'Let's blow the gig.'

"And I'd say, 'We can't blow the gig.'

"We got there just as the opening band was coming off, and we loaded the stuff in. The record company rep was there, and she said, 'We just flew in all the retailers from Canada.'

"She tells me this before a show, and I got nervous. And I shot back some tequila and hadn't eaten all day. It was just too much. When I got out there, I hit the floor. Uh-huh. And I felt really bad. I felt worse than bad.

"I got letters that were like, 'You heroin addict…'

"Shit, I've never had a needle in my arm in my fucking life. I'm not a heroin addict. It was just a lot of stress, and a lot of heat and a lot of pressure. And I just didn't handle it right."

–*JOHNETTE NAPOLITANO,* CONCRETE BLONDE

DEF LEPPARD

Arguably the hard-rock act most emblematic of the 1980s, Def Leppard has sold more than sixty-five million records, with such powerhouse works as Pyromania and Hysteria. The band from Sheffield, England, surfaced in the late 1970s as part of the new wave of British heavy metal. But the quintet really flourished as an early juggernaut of the MTV era by utilizing its collective good looks and melodic spin on heavy metal—a potent combo once dubbed "stainless steel."

CREDIT: HELEN COLLEN

I could probably go on all day because we've done so many gigs over the years. The first one that springs to mind is the Narara Festival in Australia in '84. I've never seen rain like it. It was like biblical, Noah's Ark, baseball-sized drops. It covered the place up. There was a crowd of about thirty-five thousand. Everyone left. There were only three thousand people left in the mud—honestly, three feet deep in this mud and rain. And we thought, 'Shit, we've come all the way from wherever we were at—it was our first time in Australia—we're going on!' It wasn't a bad gig, actually. It was pretty triumphant.

"Another one that springs to mind was in Switzerland, and the audience just left at the same time. We thought, 'What the fuck is going on?' Then we got hit with tear gas. Someone had let tear gas off at the gig, then it got to us at the stage. I don't know if you've been tear gassed, but it's not very cool. You can't see. They brought in cold towels and stuff to wipe our eyes. But I don't remember if we went back on…It was just some idiot in the audience goofing around…It was a mass exodus, immediately. Bizarre."

—PHIL COLLEN, DEF LEPPARD

FITZ AND THE TANTRUMS

CREDIT: MATT BECHTOLD

Few modern bands have so effortlessly captured the sound and feel of 1960s Motown hit makers better than Fitz and the Tantrums. The noticeably guitar-free unit features the emotionally charged interplay between vocalists Michael "Fitz" Fitzpatrick and Noelle Scaggs, buoyed by the stellar musicianship of saxophonist James King, bassist Joseph Karnes, keyboardist Jeremy Ruzumna and drummer John Wicks. The ensemble's 2009 full-length debut, **Pickin' Up the Pieces,** *spawned the monster single "MoneyGrabber," leading to performances on* **The Tonight Show with Jay Leno, Conan** *and* **Jimmy Kimmel Live.**

◆ ◆ ◆

"We did a whole tour through the Midwest and the Northeast when it was the dead of winter... There was one night we played in Columbus, Ohio, that was one of the greatest shows we ever did because the crowd was just raucous, and insane and into it. But as soon as I stepped out on the stoop—I had never been in an ice storm before because I'm from California—I didn't know what was going on. I had my sax on my back, stepped out on the stoop, went backward, landed on my horn and then bounced on my ass down ten steps. So that sucked...I had to get through two and a half more weeks of tour with a bad back...I had sprung on fancy Sorel snow boots. I thought I was the pimp. But they're useless against ice. I gotta get the ice-climbing gear next time we go to Ohio in the wintertime.

"But that's really not a bad gig; that was just a bad fall. Other gigs I can tell you about were from when

I did a lot of touring with hip-hop artists…We were out with the Hip-Hop Live tour in 2007. We were backing Ghostface Killah, Brother Ali and Rakim… We were in Baltimore—roughest crowd of the tour and a rough part of town. We were backstage waiting to go on. Ghostface slayed it. Brother Ali came out and did a good job, but the whole crowd was chanting, 'Rakim. Rakim. Rakim.'

"They wanted him onstage now—and he wasn't coming. Didn't show up. Twenty minutes went by, half an hour went by, forty-five minutes. Same deal. We were playing our songs, and they wanted nothing to do with that. They were booing us off the stage. Finally, the promoter had to come on and say, 'Rakim won't be making it tonight because he's stuck in traffic'—which is total bullshit. We all knew Rakim had taken the opportunity the night before to hang at his house in New York and left with not enough time to get to Baltimore.

"They started rioting. [The promoters] locked us backstage in the green room until the cops could show up and clear it out. We couldn't come out to see what was going on, but we heard everything. That was kind of surreal…I think it was full-blown rioting outside. The security couldn't handle it. There were people throwing bottles. The cops finally had to come and break it up. But they are like, 'You are not to leave this room until the situation is under control.'

"It was a good couple hours before we could leave there."

—JAMES KING, FITZ AND THE TANTRUMS

GEORGE WINSTON

George Winston is dubbed the "father of new-age music." And he's been proving his musical virility since the early 1970s, first arriving in the public eye through the iconic Windham Hill label and later with his own Dancing Cat Records. He is the rare musician who can claim to have three Platinum and four Gold records of instrumental piano music. His material ranges from his own atmospheric pieces based on seasonal cycles to records covering The Doors and Vince Guaraldi's jazz compositions for the Peanuts cartoons.

"The first time I went to Denver, with the altitude thing I kept forgetting the name of the radio station I was supposed to thank. I would say, 'I'd like to thank—what is it?' Then somebody would yell it to me. Then I'd say, 'I want to thank…' Then I'd forget it again. I forgot it four times. I was like, 'What is going on here?' I'd never had a drink in my life or a drug. I hadn't even taken aspirin. Then somebody afterward asked, 'Are you a little bit woozy?' I said I was and wasn't feeling great, either. They said, 'That's your first time with the altitude.' Good thing I didn't go to Crested Butte."

—GEORGE WINSTON

TOWER OF POWER

CREDIT: BRIAN RACHLIN

Despite a career spanning six decades, Tower of Power is still better known for its mind-boggling amount of appearances on other artists' records. The Oakland-based combo was hatched in 1968 by tenor saxophonist-vocalist Emilio Castillo and baritone saxophonist Stephen "Doc" Kupka, who continue to be the driving force behind the ten-piece ensemble. Its unmistakable horn section has backed a catalog of performers that include Elton John, Aerosmith, Little Feat, Heart, Ray Charles, The B-52's and Neil Diamond.

♦ ♦ ♦

"We played the Chesterfield Café, which was this really small bar in downtown Paris. It was extremely hot that day, like heatstroke hot. I don't know if you've ever been to Paris in the summer, but it's incredibly humid. So everybody is walking around looking like a Rorschach test. They're sweating unbelievably. And that's what it's like outside, but in the Chesterfield Café it was packed to the rafters. The stage was the size of a postage stamp. We're ten pieces with all these horns. So there's no dancing this time. We're playing, and the people are literally right in our face. There might have been some chairs in the peripheral; I couldn't see them. It was people standing shoulder to shoulder, right up to the stage. They're loving it, but it was so incredibly hot. Suffocating, you know.

"We all went on wearing shorts. We played the gig, and after there were these pools of sweat underneath everybody. When we came offstage, we all took our clothes off. I was wearing these shorts, and I wrung them out. It wasn't like a few drops came out; it was pouring. It was like I soaked them in a shower. I remember I walked across the street with a couple of the guys—by now it's nighttime and it's cooled off. But we just collapsed. We were on the ground, leaning against a building, completely drained.

"Even to this day, after all these gigs, we'll say, 'Remember the Chesterfield Café? Now that was hot!'"

—EMILIO CASTILLO, TOWER OF POWER

Siblings Sherri Dupree-Bemis, Chauntelle Dupree D'Agostino, Weston Dupree, Stacy Dupree and cousin Garron Dupree seemed to possess an obvious moniker for their band. But instead of Dupree, they went with the name Eisley—a condensed nod to Mos Eisley, the "wretched hive of scum and villainy" from Star Wars. All of the members hadn't yet graduated high school when they inked their first record deal, subsequently showcasing their dreamy, punchy pop rock as openers on Coldplay's A Rush of Blood to the Head tour. Dupree-Bemis—who recently married Say Anything singer Max Bemis—penned this story during a break from touring in her much-warmer hometown of Tyler, Texas.

EISLEY BRAVES THE SNOWPOCALYPSE

By Sherri DuPree-Bemis

"You guys should really leave tonight, they say a huge snowstorm is going to hit."

I waved off my mom's words as one of those "overly concerned" warnings mothers give in excess and opened my new books from Amazon.com that had arrived at her house (when you travel a lot, it's handy to have parents who live nearby).

As I scampered back out to my car with my arms full of crisp new comics, science fiction and fantasy novels, I never would have guessed how handy they would really be during the next few days that we would be stranded because of "snowpocalypse."

CREDIT: BOYD DUPREE

Our tour was slated to start in Albuquerque, New Mexico, which is about a twelve-hour drive from Tyler, Texas, where we all live, so we gave ourselves a two-day head start. Plenty of time, right? Nope. An ice storm had struck Texas and laid waste to the countryside during the night as we slept. It was a Texan's nightmare. Especially when you're a solid summer lover, like me.

I've lived in Texas my whole life, and until that day I could count on one hand how many times I'd seen it snow in the state. It just doesn't happen here. When it *did* snow, it was rarely "real" snow (the beautiful fluffy kind that falls wistfully across Christmas cards and makes snowball fights so much fun); it was ice. Slick, cruel and rock hard—the kind you ball up into a makeshift snowball as a kid, thinking you are going to have a "fun" snowball fight with your older sister, only to chunk it playfully at her face and give her a black eye—yes, that was me.

A few miles out of our hometown we hit the ice, and what *should* have been a two-hour drive to Dallas turned into a slipping, sliding, hazardous, anxiety attack-laden *seven*-hour drive of hell. Since it ices over so rarely in this part of the country, our state doesn't know the meaning of the words *snow* and *plow*. We nearly jackknifed our van and trailer and careened off the road numerous times. At one of the many points that we became stuck, a man in a camouflage jumpsuit and a Magnum, PI, mustache dashed out of his giant truck and began jumping on our trailer hitch with all his might trying to get us free from a snowdrift.

We were all afraid he'd slip and we'd be responsible for his death...but I'm not sure how probable "death by jumping on trailer hitch" is, so in all likelihood he was not in any real danger. Plus, with a mustache like that, you doubtless have the power to defy death.

After Magnum helped us break free, we slid on for another hour or so before we finally gave up on the journey and pulled into a hotel. We realized we would never be able to make it to the Albuquerque show at the rate we were going (your grandmother with both of her hip replacements could have outrun our tour van), so we contacted the other bands to let them know we wouldn't be there. Turns out they barely made it to the show themselves.

The following show was going to be in Tulsa, Oklahoma, two days later—just four hours from where we were camped.

In hopes of the ice thawing a bit, we sat safely for the next day and a half at the hotel surviving off ramen noodle soup and oatmeal cream pies, watching *Zombieland* and *House Hunters*—all the time a mere three hours from home, unable to get safely back and unable to move safely forward.

After what seemed a very long two days, the morning of the Tulsa show finally arrived. We packed up our remaining oatmeal cream pies and piled into the van (my two sisters, my two brothers, my cousin and I, who make up the band; my sister's husband, who tour manages; our sound man; and a partridge in a pear tree), but none of the ice had even *thought* about melting.

We managed to skate into Oklahoma safely, though the highways were littered with twisted semitrucks and numerous other cars belly up or simply abandoned in the snow. Apparently, Oklahoma had been hit just as badly as Texas, and likewise the words *snow* and *plow* were just as foreign to them as they were to us! But all went relatively well until we met a dead end about three tiny miles from the venue and had to take a shortcut through a snow-sunken neighborhood.

That is where we spent the next four hours trapped: in a shimmery, shining, completely unsplendid snowdrift the size of an Oompa-Loompa (that's all it takes, by the way).

Thank God for my books at this point.

The boys all jumped out into the sixteen-degree weather and began clawing, scraping, shoveling, kicking and swearing at the snow, trying with all their might to set us free. But with the heaviest of my brothers and cousin weighing in at about 150 (and he's six foot two), you can imagine the success we had. I suppose we could have called a tow truck, but when you're a band of starving artists (literally at this point) a $300 tow-truck bill might as well be $3,000.

At one point a couple of *completely* stoned but superkind young men overseeing the fiasco danced over (yes, danced) to try and help us out. Now I'm a big "jump in there and do what you can" kind of girl, but weighing in under 115 pounds, I would have lasted about thirty seconds before my spiderlike fingers turned into icicles and cracked off into the snow, and there would be no more playing guitar—thus no more shows. Then again, if there were no more shows, I guess there would be no more being stranded in the snow because I would be at home next to my fireplace so—hmm—something to think about!

Joking. But even between seven skinny guys, two shovels, a two-by-four board and one small bag of sand that a passerby bestowed on us, the rig wasn't going to budge.

We had already missed our soundcheck at this point and were in danger of not making it the last three miles to the venue at all, so we finally threw a couple of acoustic guitars and our Fender Rhodes into the back of the van and abandoned our trailer in the wicked drift (as well as our drummer and bassist to guard it), so that us girls could get to the venue and *at least* play an acoustic set.

Before driving off, the kind, stoned young men handed over the gift of a "jingle stick." Now I know that sounds really wrong, and I'm still not quite unsure that it *isn't*. But all I know is, one of them thrust some sort of stick device through the window with feathers and about a hundred beer caps strung from it. I believe it was meant to be a "musical" device. We were informed we could use it onstage at our show that night.

Sadly, I confess the jingle stick did not find its way into any of the songs that evening, but it was nonetheless very thoughtful of them.

After we arrived and thawed out in the venue, the boys, back in Snowzilla's neighborhood, were finally able to flag down a passerby with four-wheel drive who helped haul the trailer out. They showed up half an hour before the first band was to start. Not in enough time for us to lug all of our gear out, set up and play a full-band set, but at this point we were just glad they were safe and out of the cold—and not musiciancicles.

I can't say it was one of the *best* shows we played that night. After such a chaotic day your brain kind of goes into autopilot, and I used whatever brain waves I had left over to get through the set and try my hardest to make sure the kids singing along in the front row didn't know how distracted and worn out I felt after four days of battling Snowkenstein. Ultimately, we did have fun, and getting to meet the people afterward who had braved the storm themselves—who thanked us for coming or who had walked a mile in the blizzard because they couldn't find parking nearby—really warmed our frozen little hearts and made it all feel worth it.

So the moral of this story? Mother always knows best.

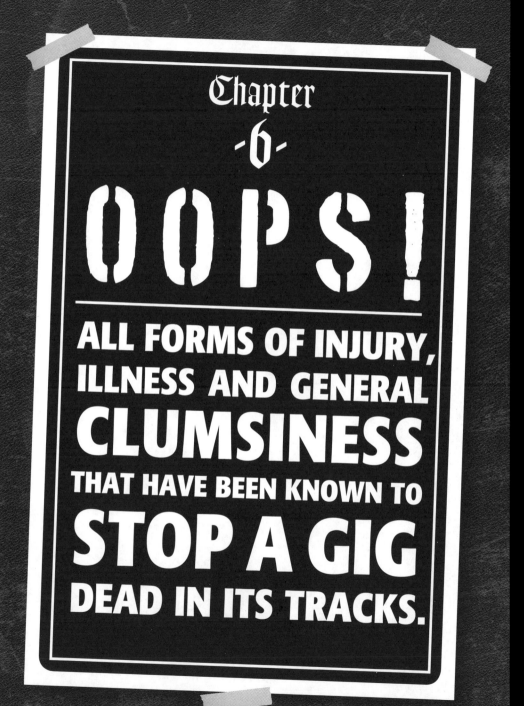

Chapter -6-

OOPS!

ALL FORMS OF INJURY, ILLNESS AND GENERAL **CLUMSINESS** THAT HAVE BEEN KNOWN TO **STOP A GIG** DEAD IN ITS TRACKS.

JANE'S ADDICTION

Jane's Addiction helped pave the way for alt rock's eventual mainstream acceptance. The Los Angeles act's first two records—Nothing's Shocking and Ritual de lo habitual—are considered among the best and most influential of the genre. Singer Perry Farrell originally disbanded his group in 1991 at the height of its popularity, but not before organizing a suitable tour as a send-off. That event became Lollapalooza, the notorious traveling music festival that was hailed as the MTV generation's Woodstock. Since then, the quartet has reformed numerous times for various albums and tours.

◆ ◆ ◆

"One time in Chicago I was kicking [heroin] really hard. So as opposed to just giving up, I faked a heart attack. I faked a heart attack, and then I faked that it was a fake. The truth of the matter is that I couldn't really stand up that well. So it might have been dramatic, but it couldn't have sounded very good. Honestly, in the day, you could get away with a lot of the drama thing."

—PERRY FARRELL, JANE'S ADDICTION

BLUE MAN GROUP

The bald-headed, indigo-skinned Blue Man Group has always mixed music into its wordless, performance-art pieces since emerging in 1987. The revolving theater troop employs freakish percussive devices that have become a visual and audio trademark. Among these are instruments made from PVC (polyvinyl chloride) pipes, "backpack tubulums," "air poles" and a "piano smasher," which is a grand piano turned on its side to expose strings that are hit with an oversized mallet.

"I threw up, so that was pretty bad. It was very early on toward the beginning of the tour. I was so thirsty I had chugged a pint of Gatorade when I got a chance to go behind the instruments. I came out with my fiberglass boat antenna and swished it around. At the end of the show we jump up and down to the beat for about a minute. So I'm jumping and I feel the Gatorade. I turn around and motion to the band to acknowledge them, then my stomach twisted and all this Gatorade just flew out of my mouth. The band just sort of looked at me. They didn't know if I was holding it in my mouth and just playing a joke. I was like, that's pretty rock and roll. It was some ridiculous flavor like kiwi-watermelon something—so that's off my list now. That was a very panicky thing. I started sweating and thinking, 'I'm just gonna lose it in front of all these thousands of people.'"

—*TOM GALASSI,* BLUE MAN GROUP

LAURIE ANDERSON

Renowned experimental musician-artist Laurie Anderson has been exploring her conceptual pieces since the late 1960s while an undergrad at Barnard College and a graduate student at Columbia University. She became something of a cult figure thanks to her piece *Duets on Ice*, in which she played a violin fitted with a tape head and a bow strung with audiotape—all while wearing ice skates with blades encased in a block of ice. The piece ended when it melted. She eventually moved into the world of recordings, leading to her minimalist 1981 single "O Superman," which hit number two on the UK charts.

"**I** was trying to stop smoking and I had the Nicoderm patch, which is basically speed. You wake up in the morning and you think, 'I'll rearrange all the furniture in the house!' So I was doing that and I had this show in Spain in a couple days, and I thought, 'I'm going to have it translated and do it in Spanish—a language I don't speak.' So it was a show with lots of words, but it also had a lot of images [projected]. I slowly read the Spanish, and by the end of the show I thought it went really well. But I looked out and every single person had gone. There was no one left in the theater. Then I walked offstage and all the production people were looking at the floor. I'm saying, 'Wasn't that great?' They were like, 'I'm working for a crazy person.' The show—which was normally about an hour— took four hours. My timing was—well, you couldn't even say it was off. It took four times longer than it normally would. It was ridiculous. Nicoderm is a powerful mood enhancer, I guess."

—LAURIE ANDERSON

JOHN MAYER

John Mayer built his initial success through a devoted grassroots following that embraced his breathy voice, complex compositions, stellar guitar chops and boyish good looks. To paraphrase Yogi Berra, Mayer was selling out shows before anybody had ever heard of him. Now armed with seven Grammy wins, the tabloid heartthrob is respected for stepping outside the sensitive songwriting of his early career to explore various genres that include blues and hip-hop.

"St. Patrick's Day, 2001. It was the absolute worst show I ever played in my life. It was at Vanderbilt University in Nashville, Tennessee. It was the worst show for a bunch of reasons: Number one, I hadn't been sleeping because I'd been recording my record. Number two, because I'd been recording my record, my sense of the lineage of my songs from beginning to end was so messed up. Everything in the studio was punched or over-dubbed or edited or moved, and I'd actually forgotten how to play straight through them. Third of all, I was getting really sick. Together it made the absolute worst experience I've ever had onstage in my life. Hopefully, that will last for the rest of my life as the worst show…Yet everyone had a memory of loving it. Then again, that was so early in my playing career, I don't think there was anything to really contrast against—except for silence."

—JOHN MAYER

12ᵀᴴ PLANET

American dubstep is a genre of electronic dance music known for its pulsating bass lines, periodic vocals and samples—and John Dadzie is one of its premier practitioners. Operating under the name 12th Planet (a reference to author Zecharia Sitchin's theories involving ancient astronauts), the producer-DJ has achieved worldwide popularity for his vigorous, original live sets. His appearances at elite festivals such as Lollapalooza and Coachella have continued to bolster his reputation as a dubstep guru.

◆ ◆ ◆

"**M**y worst gig happened when it was my twenty-second birthday…at Adrenaline [in] Orange County. I was mid-mix, and I threw up on the decks and all on myself after taking one Patrón shot…At the time I wasn't the biggest hard-alcohol drinker. I was a beer guy. My buddy was bringing me birthday shots. I thought it was going to be something that goes down smooth, and I just wasn't expecting it. I just went like, 'Bam!' You know that feeling when the Patrón hits the bottom of your stomach? Then it was just like, 'Ohhhhh…wuhhhh…' All the equipment stopped [because] I threw up on the mixer and turntables. *That's* a bad gig."

—*12TH PLANET*

CHAMBERLIN

Like the vintage analog keyboard for which it's named, Chamberlin is most comfortable providing atmosphere. The act commenced in 2010 as a partnership between singer-guitarists Mark Daly and Ethan West, who originally demoed tracks at a mountain cabin in their native Vermont. Chamberlin's tunes draw comparisons to fellow indie-folk acts such as Fleet Foxes and Bon Iver, imparting lyrics that lean toward "jealousy, despair and resentment."

◆ ◆ ◆

"**W**e left from Vermont and had to drive thirty-three hours to get to Aspen, Colorado. We opened up for Grace Potter. It was fine, but we were all exhausted. We had to continue on to the next show, which was in Wyoming up in the Tetons at this ski area. We hadn't slept in beds for four nights at that point.

"We played two shows at a festival, opening for Sharon Jones and Grace Potter. Then there was an after-party. We were running out of adrenaline but decided we'd play the after-party—it's a bar, a ski area, a lot of people would be there. The exhaustion caught up with all of us at the same time. We started playing after they'd given us free margaritas—which is the worst combination for us. The band as a whole has problems with margaritas. I bet in our rider we put 'no free margaritas' after this show.

"Basically, we were all suffering from altitude sickness at that point, too. We drove up the mountains quickly, and we'd been drinking. This is when the shit hit the proverbial fan. At the after-party show, one unnamed member of our band couldn't stand up from some combination of booze, altitude and sleep deprivation. He sat down and continued playing facing the wall. Eventually, he left the stage altogether.

"Then I got sick into a guitar case. There was nothing else around, and I had to throw up somewhere. A guitar case is actually a perfect receptacle.

"The other thing is that members of Grace Potter's band and Sharon Jones and the Dap-Kings were all at this party, and we're melting down onstage in front of them. After the certain member left the stage, we played a few Neil Young covers we didn't know and were like, 'We're done.'

"We left the stage, and we were a combination of pissed off at each other and fucked up. Then the worst part of it was we had to leave for Vermont that night to get back. That's a forty-hour drive. Somebody had stayed sober enough to get us out of there. After leaving the show, we stopped to get food somewhere in the middle of Wyoming. There were a couple of fast-food joints. Somebody was still recovering from the show and wandered off while we were at the gas station. We couldn't find them. That was a whole other fiasco that prolonged the drama.

"But we made it back fine. Nobody died. We all are better friends for it."

—ETHAN WEST, CHAMBERLIN

NADA SURF

Nada Surf is best known for its alt-rock hit "Popular." Featuring spoken lyrics culled from a 1964 dating manual, the anthem had just the right mix of irony, angst and catchiness to become an MTV staple during 1996. But it initially painted the Brooklyn-based trio (guitarist-vocalist Matthew Caws, bassist Daniel Lorca and drummer Ira Elliot) as something of a one-trick pony. Fortunately, Nada Surf followed up with the fine albums The Proximity Effect, Let Go and The Weight Is a Gift, which earned significant praise from both the mainstream and underground press.

"I've only played one show high. It was at Lehigh University. The first three songs were absolutely the worst thing I've ever done. Then the end of the show was one of the best shows ever—but at what price? Like we're playing 'Bacardi' as the third song. The middle bit has this relatively complicated classical-sounding arpeggio. I got to that part and I didn't even try and play it. I just stopped playing—'Well, that's much too complicated. I can't do that right now. Maybe later, but not right now.'"

—MATTHEW CAWS, NADA SURF

PETER FRAMPTON

CREDIT: RICHARD AARON

Few rock artists are as instantly associated with the medium of live performance as Peter Frampton. The guitarist's 1976 Frampton Comes Alive became the biggest-selling live album of all time—one of the most unexpected success stories in pop-music history. The achievement came after the British musician had established himself through five albums in the early supergroup Humble Pie, followed by four modest solo records. With Alive, Frampton became a household name, garnering Rolling Stone's Artist of the Year along with a slew of other honors. Despite these accolades, it wasn't until 2007 that Frampton won a Grammy for his instrumental album Fingerprints.

◆ ◆ ◆

"One of the worst things that's happened to me was having someone in the band who just had a bad night and wasn't playing the notes at all. This was ages ago. That was the most embarrassing thing for me—and embarrassing for him too. It was my show and it was nowhere near what it should be. I'm not going to say who it was, but it was no one who was with the band for a long time. It just blew my mind that someone could be that bad. And I came off the stage and I had welts on my face. I'd come out in hives I was so embarrassed. Musically, it's got to be right for me."

—*PETER FRAMPTON*

RUBBLEBUCKET

Brooklyn's Rubblebucket sports an overflowing bucketful of influences, with horn-laden dance material meeting indie-rock whimsy. The eight-piece act—which made its Bonnaroo debut in 2012, aided by surprise guest Foster the People—is piloted by vocalist-saxophonist Kalmia Traver and songwriter-trumpeter Alex Toth. Its revisionist version of "Michelle" recently made Paste magazine's list "Best Beatles Covers of All Time."

"**W**e were playing a small 'American festival' in New Jersey. It was a campground festival with a mix of hippies and Bruce Springsteen–loving types. At the time, we had a couple of vegans in the band, including our guitar player. Backstage, they did not have any vegan food. But what they did have was ten different choices of flavored vodkas. So instead of eating food, our guitar player grabbed a plate of tortilla chips and tons of vodka. By the time we hit the stage, he was blackout drunk.

"The venue had three HD cameras and was doing a full-on filming with a superfancy soundboard recording of the gig. At first we thought the guitar player being drunk was pretty funny. But quickly into the gig we realized he just couldn't play his parts. And that wasn't funny. The guitar parts are crucial to polyrhythmic, superlocked, funky music. We didn't have that on this night. There was one song where he started everything, and he couldn't play the part at all.

"At one point he left the stage and disappeared. Then he'd periodically come back. If you watch the video, there's a lot of footage of him sitting onstage smoking cigarettes.

"He had a microphone as well, and he kept talking nonsense to the crowd—words that didn't go together. I've never experienced any drunkenness that extreme before. It was pretty debaucherous."

—ALEX TOTH, RUBBLEBUCKET

BORGORE

After drumming for the death-metal band Shabira, Israeli musician Asaf Borger reinvented himself as Borgore. Now the love-him-or-hate-him provocation addict is at the forefront of the international dubstep scene, churning out aggressive beats that incorporate his piano and saxophone skills. Borgore's videos have logged millions of views on YouTube, and his many EPs of original, often explicit material has led to his own subgenre, called gorestep.

CREDIT: STEVEN PAHEL

"**I**n Memphis, I got food poisoning [from pizza] five minutes before the show.

"The gig was actually good. The kids had fun. But it was just me thinking I was going to the hospital after the gig. I was supposed to play an hour and a half, but I only played an hour. A few minutes before the set I started puking. The tour manager just gave me a bucket. I filled the whole bucket. Every time I turned around to puke, my video guy turned all the lights on the stage super bright so no one could look at the stage.

"I was telling [the audience] that I was sick, but they weren't fully aware that I was puking. But the stage was smelly. My dancers and my MC almost kicked the bucket. My video guy almost stepped into the bucket.

"I was delirious. I thought I was going to faint and lose control over my—how do you say in English? It's the thing that controls all your [bodily] exits. Well, I thought I'd fall on the stage, bang my head, lose control of my exits and end up in the hospital. I was counting the minutes. Every song I played I knew it meant I was closer to the end.

"I'm not sure if it was because of the pizza, but I'm sure that after the show I had no pizza in my stomach anymore."

—BORGORE

DAUGHTRY

Daughtry—although the name has yet to conjure the singular power of Hendrix, Clapton or Cobain, singer-guitarist Chris Daughtry is well on his way. The artist's torrid growl and sweeping power ballads such as "Home" have made Daughtry and his band of the same moniker one of the top-selling rock acts of the past decade (his eponymous debut was Billboard's number-one album of 2007). Not bad for a fourth-place finisher in the fifth season of American Idol.

"**U**nfortunately, it was near my hometown. It was Charlotte, North Carolina. I was so sick that I sounded like a barking dog the entire show. The crowd had to sing most of it. They were like a support group. Looking back, it was a show I probably should have canceled and come back through on the next tour. That was one I felt like crawling under a rock... The crowd was great, though. It would have been horrible if they would have been booing or throwing stuff. It's certainly a debilitating feeling when you can't use your main instrument."

—CHRIS DAUGHTRY

ANTHRAX

New York's Anthrax became part of the "big four"—flanking Megadeth, Metallica and Slayer—that ushered thrash metal from the underground to Platinum success during the 1980s. The band was among the first to intersect rap and metal with the seminal Public Enemy collaboration (and tour) Bring the Noise. Although the evolving lineup has incorporated several dozen members over the decades, guitarist Scott Ian and drummer Charlie Benante have appeared on every Anthrax album.

◆ ◆ ◆

"We were in Osaka, Japan. We often switch instruments in the first encore. I would play guitar. Scott [Ian] or Joey [Belladonna] would play drums. I remember in Japan they were throwing things onstage that night—just toys and whatever. During part of the song I went over to tell [guitarist] Danny Spitz about someone throwing a Batman thing to us. When I leaned in to whisper in his ear, he swung his head back really fast and cracked me in the nose. I saw stars. I had to go sit down for a minute because I thought I was gonna pass out. Turns out my nose was very definitely broken. It was bleeding everywhere. You heard this big reaction from the crowd, like, 'Oooooh, nooooo. That's so sad.' But I was able to go back out and finish the last song before they took me to the hospital. Wasn't the first time I broke my nose. But it was the first time in front of an audience."

—*CHARLIE BENANTE,* ANTHRAX

Nobody has concocted a better brew of vintage country and punk-rock attitude than Nashville's BR549. Started in 1993 by singer-guitarist Chuck Mead and drummer Shaw Wilson, the honky-tonk act spent years playing for tips as house band at the bar and clothing store Robert's Western Wear. Performances on **Late Show with David Letterman** *and* **Conan** *ensued, as did seven albums and three Grammy nominations. Recently, Mead bridged Nashville and Broadway as music director for the Tony Award–winning musical* **Million Dollar Quartet,** *a fictionalized account of the famous 1956 jam session involving Elvis Presley, Johnny Cash, Jerry Lee Lewis and Carl Perkins. Mead also contributed new material to the show and produced the original cast album.*

BR549'S STOMACH-TURNING
WORST SHOW

By Chuck Mead

CREDIT: JIM HERRINGTON

It was New Year's Eve, and BR549 had a gig in Odessa, Texas, at this huge metal armory-type building. We had been off for Christmas and hadn't seen one another for a couple of weeks after virtually spending nearly every waking hour together for months on the road.

As we were driven to the local radio station, everyone was in good spirits. It carried over to the radio performance—lots of snappy dialogue, good songs, happy DJs. We had already set up at the venue so we were free to join some of the sponsoring radio station people for a dinner at a local eatery. On the way over to the restaurant, I started feeling weird—a little ill, but I thought food would help. I remember it being an animated dinner with more snappy dialogue and some spicy catfish.

At some point the bandmate I was rooming with (we almost always shared rooms) had invited a couple of the hipper guys from the radio station to visit us at our hotel room and bring some "party favors." He told them our room number and said, "We'll see you all before the gig."

So we went back to the hotel and on the way there, I started feeling really bad: splitting headache, double vision, et cetera. I just wanted to lie down until we had to leave for the gig at 9 p.m. I think we were supposed to start around 9:30 p.m. or 10 p.m., and the radio guys were going to come over and party and then we'd all go over to the gig. I thought surely I could get my shit together by then.

But as I lay there trying to recharge, I began feeling worse and worse. At that point I knew my body would eventually expel the sickness somehow.

Then it started.

First I tried to get the poison out by sitting on the toilet.

It was definitely coming out in its most disgusting version. I got back to my bed thinking it might pass when suddenly there was a knock on our door. It was the radio guys. It was only 7:15 p.m. It seems they misunderstood. They thought we said to come over at 7:15, when really that was our room number. So now I'm lying there trying to keep it all together in a roomful of radio guys smoking, drinking, talking and laughing.

Then the puking followed.

Now I was alternately puking and shitting amid a cloud of smoke and cheap champagne, which was making things much worse.

I kept hearing distant voices. "Is he going to be all right?" "Wow, that really smells."

This went on for what seemed like hours until one more visit to the bathroom clogged the toilet. Now the room was filled with smoke, and the toilet was bound up with puke and diarrhea. I think that's when the radio guys left.

So I got my show-date suit on and lay there on the bed looking like a corpse at a wake until it was time to go. On the way over they put me on the window side of the van, of course, and immediately upon arrival at the gig, I was puking in a corner of the parking lot. I think it was at that point I told our tour manager that he should set up a trash can behind my amp in case I needed it.

"Seriously?" he asked.

"Do I look like I'm kidding?" I said as I spit a little bile onto the gravel.

We got in there, and the place was packed. It was New Year's Eve, and everyone was in a fine mood and rowdy and ready to go. I remember being in some sort of trance standing onstage as they introduced us. I just wanted to "maintain." My head was splitting, and my stomach distressed. I was delirious and playing on 100 percent autopilot.

About forty minutes into the show, we kicked off "Crazy Arms," a song on which I sang lead. Halfway through the first verse I knew I was going to hurl. All I had to do was hold it in until the fiddle break. We got to the chorus and I glanced over to see our fiddle player plucking on his instrument, looking at the monitor guy and shrugging because there was no sound.

Since I'm the only other lead instrument in our band, if there's no fiddle to take the break, I have to do a guitar ride. But I was about to puke. I was picturing me splashing vomit all over the two-steppers at the front of the stage and then getting my ass kicked by some big Texan because I peppered his wife with chunks of spicy catfish on New Year's Eve.

Thankfully, at the last second, the fiddle came back. As I finished the final lines of the chorus, I spun around to the back of my amp and let it fly.

Our drummer set up in back of all the amps to have the perfect view of events taking place behind the rest of us. He told me the stream of vomit made a perfect arc (like a chunky rainbow) from my mouth to the trash can.

I had time to wipe my mouth and then get back up to the mic for the second verse.

I finished the show somehow, and while the other guys had a meet and greet, I puked one more time in the parking lot for good measure. When we got back to the hotel, our tour manager set us up in a new room that had a toilet that wasn't clogged with my disgusting discharge, and I promptly went to bed.

I was in a warm, dry, dark, safe place snug inside my bed, shivering a little, listening to all my bandmates and the radio guys partying down the hall. I turned the TV on so I could drift off to sleep, and the movie *Back to School* came on.

And that's how Rodney Dangerfield saved my life one New Year's Eve.

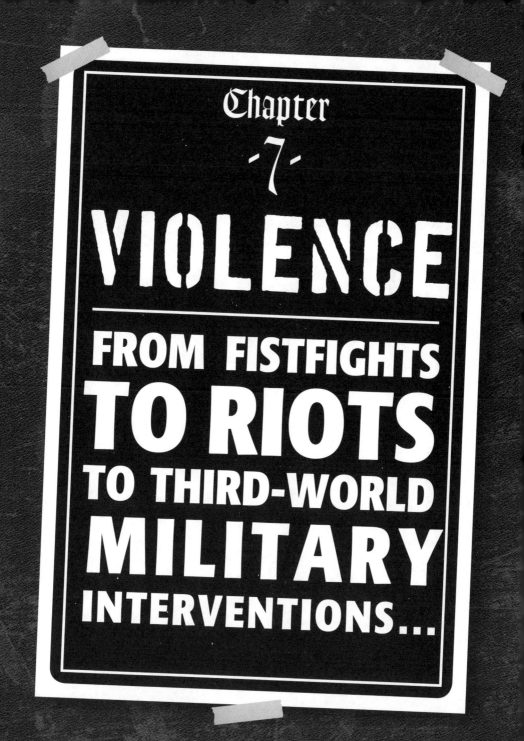

Chapter ·7·

VIOLENCE

FROM FISTFIGHTS TO RIOTS TO THIRD-WORLD MILITARY INTERVENTIONS...

THE SEX PISTOLS

CREDIT: HELEN COLLEN

When the first line ever written by a band is "I am an antichrist," that's a lot to live up to. And though the images of singer Johnny Rotten, bassist Sid Vicious, drummer Paul Cook and guitarist Steve Jones in ripped T-shirts, dyed hair and sporting safety-pin jewelry look more contemporary than shocking by today's standards, in 1977 England they were the closest thing to Satan the country had seen. When the quartet's classic single "God Save the Queen" was released, the BBC banned it. When it went to number one anyway, the slot was left blank rather than admitting which artist occupied the top position. But to modern audiences, The Sex Pistols are regarded as the greatest and most influential punk band of all time, and their lone record, **Never Mind the Bollocks,** *is deemed an irrefutable classic.*

◆ ◆ ◆

"One has really stuck in my mind as my worst gig scenario. I remember it well because it was my fortieth birthday on the Pistols reunion in '96. It was my fortieth birthday, and I thought it was going to be a great day. It was in Belgium actually, by the seaside somewhere. We got on the train from London to Belgium, the Eurostar that went to Brussels. I was going to keep it quiet, but someone mentioned it was my birthday. This was nine o'clock in the morning, so it kind of gave everyone the excuse to get the champagne out. You can guess that by the time we arrived in Belgium, everyone was really tanked up... Basically, it just turned into a nightmare. By the time we took to the stage, John had completely lost his voice. Consequently, nobody could hear what was going on onstage. I don't think anything was coming out of the PA, vocal-wise. Then it turned into total chaos; it got worse. I don't know what happened, but there was a mass brawl between security and people actually fighting onstage. I think someone tried to attack John, and he started hitting him with a microphone. I remember a stretcher coming onstage as well.

"Somebody was knocked out. There was blood spilt onstage, and there was fighting going on. It just seemed to escalate…We were still playing away while somebody was being carried off on a stretcher—one of the security guys. It was just one of those gigs, and I was expecting to have a really good day for my birthday…It was a classic rock-and-roll gig, I guess. What was the most miraculous thing about it all was that at the end we actually got an encore. People wanted more!"

—PAUL COOK, THE SEX PISTOLS

JOE SATRIANI

CREDIT: CHRISSIE GOODWIN

Joe Satriani first came to prominence as a guitar teacher to the stars, with Steve Vai, Metallica's Kirk Hammett and Counting Crows' David Bryson as pupils. Soon, however, the teacher gained notoriety of his own, following the 1987 release of his Platinum-selling Surfing with the Alien. *Although he's spent time filling in as a member of noted bands (Deep Purple) and as a sideman for other stars (Mick Jagger and Alice Cooper), Satriani tours nearly every year with G3, a concert event he founded that partners him with other renowned six-stringers such as Queen's Brian May, King Crimson's Robert Fripp and Journey's Neal Schon.*

◆ ◆ ◆

"That would be the Malaysian show…It [started] four hours late, so we went on at four in the morning. And it was in this stadium that holds one hundred thousand people. But it was raining, so there were only about two thousand people there. Before us there was Jethro Tull, there was Sugar Ray…Toto—just the weirdest group of bands ever. It was a two-day festival. Anyway, someone wakes me up at 3:30 a.m. and says, 'You're going on at 4 a.m.'

"So I get down there, I'm in the middle of the second song—which is 'Satch Boogie'—and the [Malaysian] army comes onstage with machine guns. They threaten to put us in jail unless we stop immediately. So I put down my guitar, I picked up my backpack, and I left the stadium.

"I have no idea [why they needed me to stop], but I

didn't argue. When you're in a country like that and they show up onstage with weapons—you know, I came packed because I knew from experience that sometimes you gotta be ready. So I literally put on my backpack and gave my guitar to my tech.

"I said, 'Put it in the case and come with me now.'

"Then we got in a car and left, and three hours later I was at the airport flying home."

—*JOE SATRIANI*

TOOL

Grammy-winning, multi-Platinum-selling quartet Tool has perfected what Rolling Stone calls "a primal sound as distinct as it is disturbing." The Los Angeles band (singer Maynard James Keenan, guitarist Adam Jones, bassist Justin Chancellor and drummer Danny Carey) assembled in 1990 and has since become one of the godfathers of the progressive metal movement.

"We played up at Boise, Idaho, one time. It was an outdoor thing and quite a few people showed up. I remember this horrible feeling looking at the crowd where all these malicious, skinhead psychos showed up and started beating people up to our music. We had to cut the set short out of fear that someone was going to get beat to death. That was pretty grim…I remember it being a tough decision. We just got in a huddle onstage and said, 'Man, what are we gonna do? Every time we start playing a song all these fists just start flying.'"

–DANNY CAREY, TOOL

MIKE FINNIGAN

Mike Finnigan was a nineteen-year-old student at the University of Kansas when he became the proud owner of a Hammond B3 organ. Since then he's transformed into one of the premier purveyors of the instrument. His collaborations have ranged from blues greats Buddy Guy and Etta James to pop stars Peter Frampton and Rod Stewart, to rockers Jane's Addiction and Poison. He also spent years touring with Crosby, Stills and Nash. But he is most celebrated for contributing organ to the tracks "Rainy Day, Dream Away" and "Still Raining, Still Dreaming" on Jimi Hendrix's classic Electric Ladyland.

◆ ◆ ◆

"When I was starting out I used to play in nightclubs for like weeks at a time. You'd go somewhere and play for two weeks in a club, and then they might pick up an option and hold you over. I remember being forcibly held over by a mobbed-up joint—guys that were part of the broken-nose club…I was a young guy, and these guys were legitimately gangsters. They were like the real thing. They weren't like just faux tough guys, they were really mobbed up in those days. Like in Youngstown, Ohio, it was like Crimetown, USA. The guy who owned it was a known guy.

"I told him in advance we had another commitment—it was just before Christmas—back in Kansas City, and we'd been out in the Midwest and the East for a couple of months.

"I said, 'There's no option on this. We can only do the two weeks.'

"He said, 'Fine.'

"Then after a couple of days he was like, 'We really like your band. I'm thinking about holding you over.'

"I said, 'Don't forget, I told you we had this commitment.'

"Then a couple of days later he said, 'I've decided to hold you over.'

"I said, 'But what about…'

"He said, 'Kid, you don't get it. You're staying!'

"[So we stayed another] two weeks."

—*MIKE FINNIGAN*

HENRY ROLLINS

Henry Rollins is a modern Renaissance man—the type of person who's achieved success in so many different fields that to define him by only one is not just lazy but mildly insulting. The musician, actor, writer, poet, columnist, VJ, television host and pop-culture luminary first gained fame in 1981 as the frontman for the seminal California punk band Black Flag. With few exceptions, Rollins seems to be the rare singer who has created a cottage industry around his everyday voice. Whatever the scenario, the performer can never be accused of being dull.

"There have been a few. Not because we sucked, because I've never been onstage with a band that was high. Equipment failure was detrimental at times. In Singapore, everything basically blew up onstage; everything went poof. We had to play through the PA. No amps onstage, just plugged in direct. It sounded awful. One time in Austria in 1983 there was a riot inside the venue. The police came in. The fans beat up the cops. The fans beat up the bouncers. A guy punched me and laid me out on the ground. That gig was like, 'How are we gonna get through this? No one seems to be interested in music. They're just interested in beating the crap out of everyone, including us.'"

—HENRY ROLLINS

TRANSLATOR

San Francisco was the physical setting for Translator's ascent to popularity in the early 1980s, but musically the group owed more to British new-wave influences. Led by singer-guitarist Steve Barton, the quartet that also includes guitarist Robert Darlington, bassist Larry Dekker and drummer Dave Scheff rode its signature tune, the moody, entrancing "Everywhere That I'm Not," into a pervasive underground hit. The band continues to record and perform with its original lineup intact.

"There was a gig in Baton Rouge, Louisiana, probably in about 1982. We got to the club, and the first tip-off something was amiss was the guy who greeted us had these two snarling Dobermans.

"We were like, 'Hello?'

"He said, 'Don't worry. There's only some kind of people they don't like.'

"OK. Fine. Whatever that meant.

"So we're playing the gig, and there's this girl at the front of the stage who was either reaching up to touch us or throwing things. I don't remember. But this two-hundred-pound bouncer guy tackled her and threw her out of the club. I'm sure we said something onstage about it.

"But then at the end of the gig—and this is what makes it really memorable—our road manager went to the office to get paid. She was this fantastic woman named Christine; it was really unusual to have a road manager who was a woman back then.

"She went to the office and said, 'All right, that was a great show. We're getting ready to leave, so let's figure out the money.'

"The guy opened the drawer, took out a gun and put it on the table.

"He said, 'There's only two things I hate more than women.'

"She came out of the office white as a ghost and said, 'Get in the van. Let's get the hell out of here.'

"She told us what happened. Then when we got to the hotel, she said this club owner intimated that he and a few of his buddies were going to come by and 'take care of us.' I don't know why he didn't like us, but she insisted we get the hell out of there.

"I heard later from other people 'that happened to us.' I think the owner tried to intimidate people. It probably worked a lot of the time. But we found out afterward, to her credit, Christine stood up to him by saying, 'Give me the money and I'll get out of your face.'

"Believe it or not, he actually paid her."

—*STEVE BARTON,* TRANSLATOR

LOS LONELY BOYS

Guitarist Henry Garza, bassist Jojo Garza and drummer Ringo Garza began touring as grade schoolers while backing their father, Ringo Garza Sr., a conjunto musician who came to prominence in The Falcones. Eventually, the younger Garzas struck out on their own as Los Lonely Boys. Upon the release of a 2004 self-titled debut, the Texas trio began racking up hit singles and Grammy nods with their fusion of Tex-Mex rock and guitar-driven blues.

◆ ◆ ◆

"**M**an, it's tough to recap and recall the worst gig—there are so many of them that went south. Basically, when we first started out, I would have to say that was one of the worst gigs. We were doing a show in…I think it was Big Springs, Texas. We were playing a show with a conjunto band named Michael Salgado. They were playing, and they were kind enough to let our dad and us play with their stuff. We got up on the stage, and while we were playing, somebody shot one of [their] members. Our dad's theory of music was, 'Never stop no matter what's going on! Don't stop!' At first we didn't realize what was going on. We just saw a big commotion and heard the sound, but we were still going along. There was pepper gas flying everywhere. It was a big crowd, a big fight, and everything started breaking out…So we're looking at each other and were like, 'We should stop.' We vacated the premises as quick as we could. We didn't want no more bullets flying."

—HENRY GARZA, LOS LONELY BOYS

JEFFERSON STARSHIP

After a nine-year run as one of the pioneering psychedelic acts of the 1960s, Jefferson Airplane changed its name to Jefferson Starship and began a chart-topping ride that continues to this day—give or take a few years' hiatus. The Bay Area act forged its prolific career through classic-rock staples ("Jane," "Miracles," "Find Your Way Back") and dubious commercial hits ("We Built This City"). Although the lineup changes occur so frequently as to be almost comical, the band's arena-rock legacy is hard to dispute.

"**W**e were playing a gig in Germany at the Loreley Amphitheater [in 1978]. The Beach Boys and Chicago had canceled out back-to-back shows at this place, and people were pissed off. Half the crowd was German and the other half were American Marines. There were people in the crowd with gasoline cans. The first band had already played, and they figured the show was really going to go on this time. But Grace [Slick] had diarrhea and was throwing up. She wasn't going to go on. They asked me to go out to make the announcement.

"I said, 'You've got to be crazy. I'm not going to go out there. They're going to kill me.'

"So [keyboardist David] Freiberg said he'd go out there. There was dead silence when he said, 'We'll make the gig up, but Grace is deathly ill.'

"I was standing next to one of my roadies by my drums, and a Heineken bottle came flying through the air. It hit him in the head, and he went down like a bowling pin.

"Then a full-bore riot ensued. The Marines were fighting with the Germans. There was military there and police. One of the Germans was drunk and had a broken bottle, and he was coming up to one of the regular German police. And the policeman took his gun out and was going to waste the guy right there. It was Altamont all over again.

"A military policeman said, 'You don't have to do that.'

"He pushed the policeman's gun down with his stick and said, 'All you have to do is this!'

"And he hit [the drunk guy] over the head with his stick."

—*JOHNY BARBATA,* JEFFERSON STARSHIP

Ian MacKaye founded seminal hardcore punk act Minor Threat and equally influential label Dischord Records in 1980 when he was only eighteen years old. But it was seven years later that the do-it-yourself musician developed his definitive act, Fugazi. Along with fellow Washington, DC, singer-guitarist Guy Picciotto, drummer Brendan Canty and bassist Joe Lally, Fugazi fashioned an ever-shifting style more rhythmically driven than that of their contemporaries. Pounding guitars gave way to hypnotic patterns that constantly grappled between louds and softs. MacKaye's and Picciotto's dissimilar voices alternated lead chores, highlighting words weighted toward political or social commentary. Fugazi has been on an "indefinite hiatus" since 2002. In the interim, MacKaye has issued three albums with The Evens, a duo he devised with his drummer wife, Amy Farina. MacKaye's story is culled from several lengthy phone interviews about the topic.

FUGAZI UNDER SIEGE IN WARSAW!

By Ian MacKaye

This is not necessarily the worst gig. There are different ideas about what tends to be good or bad. But often adversity is what makes a gig great. So, in fact, this is not a bad gig. We just found ourselves in the middle of a completely insane situation.

In my mind, some of the worst gigs I ever played were in front of audiences where I felt like we could do no wrong and therefore didn't have to try to do anything right. I didn't feel good at the end of it; I basically felt like we could have been terrible and people still would have said, "You're brilliant." That doesn't move the ball.

But the story I'm going to tell you is about a particular gig Fugazi played in 1990. It was a gig that happened in circumstances that were completely unmanageable, it got completely out of control, and it was a complete surprise.

It was our first time to Poland. We had played through Scandinavia. We did a show in Sweden. The next day we took a ferryboat to the north of Poland to a town called Pila. It was a really good gig. People were dancing together. It was sort of like playing in a discotheque. There was a nice energy.

The next night we played a university in Warsaw. Very nice people were putting the show on. They were college kids. We got there and it was a beautiful room, filled with wood— which is always a very positive thing for sound in our book. We soundchecked. We were in good spirits. They had prepared a dinner for us down at a dorm house about two blocks away on the campus. We had a rented van from Holland with us, and we took that down and parked it behind the building. We had all our worldly possessions in the van, so we were very keen to keep our eye on it at all times. In Poland and other Eastern European countries, there had been a lot of reports of van theft, so we were nervous about it.

We met a bunch of university students. Some of them spoke English, which was great because we spoke no Polish.

We were grateful for their ability to communicate with us. They made dinner for us. Everything was nice. At some point I thought, "I'm going to have a nap." Before showtime I like to stretch out for ten minutes.

Later, I heard talking outside the room, and one of the band members came in and said, "The promoters just came down and said we've got a problem with some skinheads. You guys stay here. Don't come to the venue until we come get you."

We decided to stay there. It was not that unusual, so I went back to my nap. Skinheads were sort of the bane of our existence in the late 80s and early 90s. They caused a lot of problems in all countries. I was a little surprised to hear about Polish skinheads. This was shortly after [Poland] had left the Soviet bloc. But when you think about it, it makes sense. Skinheads tended to be very right-wing people, and that was a very hard push to the right when the socialist governments started to retreat.

About five minutes later there was even more of a stir. Someone came in and said, "They want us at the venue right now. Get up. We need to get up there!"

I got up and started getting our stuff together, and suddenly I heard the roar of a crowd coming down the street— the sound of yelling and windows breaking. Basically, the students had gotten into a fight with the skinheads because the students said, "You can't come to the gig." Then the skinheads attacked. But, really, skinheads were only there to attack anyway. There were apparently about a hundred of them that night.

This was still in the late afternoon before the doors to the venue had opened. The students came running at us, chased by this army of skinheads. They ran into the house, and then it was just a full-on assault against the house. My brother Alec was on the front porch when he saw the skinheads come running up. One of the skinheads jumped up on a porch railing and kicked my brother in the face and almost put his head through a window.

At this point all the Polish students were hysterically running around. No one had time to speak English with us, so we couldn't figure out what the hell was going on. I understand it now. But at the time all I knew was that the windows were breaking and there was an army of skinheads out front attacking the building. The students bolted all the doors and jammed them up with chairs, and skinheads were trying to kick their way inside. My thinking was, "We need to get out of here, and we need to get *the van* out of here."

If the van was destroyed, we were ruined. Our tours generally were many, many shows in row and that meant a lot of driving. If you were to miss one show, it would really screw you up, because you were suddenly twelve to fifteen hours away from somewhere instead of eight hours away.

And we were in Poland. Who knew if the van could even be fixed? Also, there would be nothing to fix if the van was burned to the ground.

We all got together and crawled out a window. Everybody got in the van but me. We could hear the fighting going on out front, and we didn't want to risk going back out in the street. Behind these dorms there were grassy lawns, so the van drove with its lights off through the lawns behind the houses and toward the venue. I would run up to the edge of the buildings and look around the gaps, then wave the van through.

Then we got up to the venue, where we had all the gear, so we weren't going to just leave it. A few of us got out and said to the van, "Just go." So they headed to central Warsaw and just drove around. At this point there were busloads of military police with white batons and gloves and helmets. The fighting was down the street at this point, but it was making its way back. We went into the venue, and I remember there were people on the floor with their teeth knocked out. There were all these terribly injured people lying all around. It looked like a casualty ward.

The police finally got everybody settled down and the fighting stopped. Then there was the discussion like, "Is this gig going to happen?" Our position was, "We came to play music. We're not interested in skinheads deciding that we can't, but ultimately it's your venue and your situation."

They wanted to do the gig.

The show started, and there was a handful of skinhead kids who were still trying to come into the gig. They weren't the ones in the middle of the fray, but they were connected, and the promoters wouldn't let them in. Finally the promoters said, "If you come in and start any trouble, then we'll have you arrested. But to make sure you don't, you have to leave your ID papers with us."

In Poland you had to always carry ID. So the skinheads agreed.

The show itself was pretty great. There was a lot of anger because people were very frustrated about the situation. A lot of times people got on the mic and would yell stuff. But I felt like, "That's the point of music. That's why we're here. We're not going to let violence derail that."

Unbeknownst to all of us, the promoters were busily photocopying all the IDs while the show was on. They used those photocopies to put together a class-action lawsuit and took all those kids to court.

It was an epic gig, I have to say. Coming up with punk rock, through the American punk hardcore scene, then with Fugazi, dealing with the thug repercussions of that explosive moment, I've seen an awful lot of fighting, really insane stuff. But I don't think I've ever experienced anything on that scale...

I think it was even more underscored by the fact we weren't able to communicate. My strongest power is my ability to communicate. I've waded into so many crazy situations just talking to people. I don't have any problem with that. I have walked twelve to fifteen white-power skinheads out of a venue and given them all their money back, discussing and arguing with them all the way. But I can't discuss or argue with people whose language I don't speak and whose grievance I don't understand or know about.

I was just taking a nap.

Chapter
-8-
IT'S ALL GOOD

EVEN WHEN THINGS FALL APART, PERFORMERS CAN FIND SOMETHING POSITIVE IN THE EXPERIENCE.

TORI AMOS

Poised somewhere between vulnerable debutante and femme fatale, Tori Amos is an odd mosaic. Her records are entangled, diverse offerings of highly skilled piano and studio wizardry that have managed to deposit some of the most unusual material ("God," "Cornflake Girl") ever on commercial radio. Her concerts often just feature Amos solo, perched as a terra-cotta-haired torch singer whose intellect is as promising as her libido. Amos has generated a devout fan base, fueled in part by her mesmerizing, intimate live shows.

"It was during the taping of my MTV *Unplugged* performance [in 1996]…What happened was I just couldn't harness the energy. And I got really mad at myself because I couldn't harness it. And I do this every night and I can usually harness something, and I couldn't understand why. What was wrong? What was I missing here? So I walked off [crying].

"It was the best thing I could have done because what I did was I acknowledged what the truth was—and the truth was I wasn't harnessing it; for whatever reason it wasn't happening. Because I acknowledged it, it gave me power. It gave me my strength back again. It's funny that in that moment of 'this is a mess,' you begin to kind of find the pearls.

"So when I walked offstage I went down to the dressing room and just was pacing.

"My tour manager said, 'So I guess that's it then. Should we order some food? Should we book a restaurant?'

"I said, 'What are you talking about?'

"He said, 'That's it then. You've obviously finished for the night.'

"I said, 'Not necessarily. I'm just pacing right now.'

"He said, 'OK. I'll pace with you.'

"We started pacing beneath the MTV thing.

"Then my soundman came in and said, 'What's going on? It sounds fucking great out there…I'm telling you, it sounds better than most of your shows.'

"Then my [lighting director] came down and said, 'Something just doesn't feel right. I can't put my finger on it.'

"Then my tour manager looked at my LD and they looked back at each other. And they go, 'Hang on a minute. Give us five seconds.'

"They walked outside the room and came back in smiling and said, 'The lights are up. We're going to bring the lights down.'

"For seven hundred shows over the five years [prior to that], I'd played with the lights down. So all the lights were up to catch the audience, and I felt like somebody was watching me take a shower. So they dimmed the lights, and I felt better. By that point because I'd made the choice to stop it and make some changes, I felt like I began again. And I turned the whole show around."

—TORI AMOS

INCUBUS

Contrived in 1991 while merely scruffy high school students, Incubus has gone from a commonplace funk-metal outfit to one of the more ambitious rock acts to achieve radio dominance. With multi-Platinum albums to its credit that feature perennial singles such as "Nice to Know You," "Wish You Were Here" and "Drive," the Los Angeles five-piece (powered by founding singer Brandon Boyd, guitarist Mike Einziger and drummer José Pasillas) incorporates heavy guitar riffs and turntable club sounds when putting a new spin on a weathered style.

"**T**he worst show that we've ever played was probably in a snowboard park on a piece of plywood. That was probably the worst show we've ever played, and we've played a few really bad ones…[That was] in 1993…and nobody cared that we were there. We were playing on a piece of plywood with no PA. Our singer Brandon [Boyd] had to sing out of a bass amp. It was funny. We were told there was going to be a stage and a PA and we were going to get paid and all this stuff. We didn't get paid, but we got free burritos and we thought that was cool."

—*MIKE EINZIGER, INCUBUS*

THE WALLFLOWERS

The Wallflowers' frontman Jakob Dylan is, of course, the son of legendary troubadour Bob Dylan. Since 1992, the younger Dylan has issued nearly as many albums of fresh material as his father, occasionally outselling the elder songwriter. (The Wallflowers' 1996 effort Bringing Down the Horse moved four million copies.) Dylan's Los Angeles quartet is known for a radio-friendly blend of alternative roots rock, characterized by the Grammy-winning single "One Headlight."

"It takes all kinds as they say. The shows where there isn't anybody there, it just doesn't get worse than that. So as long as people are there, any type of fiasco that goes wrong, it's all part of it. I've played at every type of show possible. I've played with some horrible people, like as an opener. When we were younger you got times when you look back and wish you weren't in the place that you were. I did fall on my back in Osaka, Japan, once. Thankfully, it was the end of the show and I just happened to fall back and step over a monitor. It was a great finale, and thankfully I couldn't read the papers to read about it so I wasn't embarrassed."

–JAKOB DYLAN, THE WALLFLOWERS

THAT 1 GUY

CREDIT: OLIVIER OSWALD

Despite the stage name That I Guy, Mike Silverman is proud that he utilizes as much gear onstage as an entire band. Silverman is best known for performing on a gigantic steel instrument of his own design that he affectionately calls the magic pipe, which is shaped like a harp that Dr. Seuss might envision. Each pipe has its own string: One is pitched high, the other low, and both are played in a percussive manner—oh, and smoke billows out the top. A classically trained upright bass player, Silverman paid his dues in the California jazz scene before reinventing himself as That I Guy. He has since expanded his skills to include bizarre instruments known as the magic boot and the magic saw. In 2008, he released a collaborative CD under the name The Frankenstein Brothers with avant-garde guitarist Buckethead.

◆ ◆ ◆

"I played at this country-western bar for this country-western radio station in Florida. The guy had seen me at another gig and thought I'd be great for this thing. It was a welcome-home party for this big country star who was going to be the new morning DJ. It was a party for all the listeners, so it was packed with country-music fans. And I've got nothing against country music. I just showed up and thought, 'I'm so out of my element here.' Not a single person had any idea who I was. I didn't think anybody knew what to expect. I got up there to play, and it was the first time I was really scared. They were all staring at me like, 'What the hell is this guy doing? Who is this dude? Where is he from? He ain't from around here, that's for sure.' It was a little, weird town, too—a funny little city that was not even on the map. It was packed and I was scared to death. But by the end, they were really, really friendly. It was a great lesson for me. It made me realize that people just want to check out and see good music. And if you can play all right and kind of get to them, then they're gonna dig it. It doesn't really matter geographically. If you're playing from your heart, it's gonna reach folks."

—*MIKE SILVERMAN,* **THAT 1 GUY**

AIMEE MANN

Singer-songwriter Aimee Mann first had to fight to free herself from the glossy image of her post-new-wave band 'Til Tuesday, which won MTV's Best New Artist Award in 1985 on the strength of its hit "Voices Carry." Then she was tied up in court for years by a bankrupt record label that prevented her from releasing solo records. But the musician persevered, crafting a string of records that earned her both Grammy and Oscar nominations along the way, most notably for her work on the Paul Thomas Anderson epic Magnolia.

"I remember playing a show at the Troubadour [in Los Angeles], where there was something wrong with the monitors and I kept hearing a really loud, weird rumbling noise onstage. I felt like I was singing so poorly that I offered to reimburse the audience. It was kind of a fun show, and people in the audience were like, 'No. It was a great show.' But the onstage sound was so weird. Nobody took me up on the offer…I almost like when stuff goes bad because it gives you something to work with. It may give you the opportunity for comedy or to just goof around—to do something that's not just playing a set. I can't really think of a time where I was totally miserable. I've played shows where I was sick. But audiences are just very supportive if you come out and try your best."

—AIMEE MANN

THE PRESIDENTS OF THE UNITED STATES OF AMERICA

While the 1990s were politically synonymous with Bill Clinton, the decade's music scene was equally receptive to The Presidents of the United States of America. The multi-Platinum band racked up quirky rock hits such as "Lump," "Peaches" and "Kitty," and it provided the version of "Cleveland Rocks" that served as the theme song to TV's The Drew Carey Show. The Seattle trio (bassist-vocalist Chris Ballew, drummer Jason Finn and newish guitarist Andrew McKeag) is equally remembered for its witty, ninja-filled videos that ruled MTV.

There was a show at a hockey rink in Medford, Oregon, where we got there and the guys putting on the show were like out of a movie. They were just trying to get in and make a quick buck in the concert promotions business. They didn't have any resources or anything. They were literally there to grab the money and run away—which they did. So we were left with this dark, leaky skate rink with a really angry manager and hundreds of kids who had just been ripped off. So we basically played a benefit that night. That was a Spinal Tap moment. But as far as bad shows musically, it doesn't happen. We're too good for that. When things go wrong, like equipment or tuning, that makes the show stronger. We excel at going off-map, off-script. It's easy with a three-piece band and to have a guy like Chris [Ballew] in front who's brilliant when he just starts winging it. That's why there is never a dull moment at a Presidents' show."

–JASON FINN, **THE PRESIDENTS OF THE UNITED STATES OF AMERICA**

CHELY WRIGHT

Kansas native Chely Wright first earned her place in Nashville's elite after being named Best New Female Vocalist in 1994 by the Academy of Country Music. She followed up on her early promise in 1999 with the number-one country hit "Single White Female." In 2001, she even landed on **People** *magazine's list "50 Most Beautiful People." But she made national headlines recently when she came out as a lesbian—a declaration that caused major ripples within the country-music industry and the world of pop culture. The announcement coincided with the release of a 2011 memoir titled* **Like Me.**

◆ ◆ ◆

"**B**efore I had a record deal, when I had a band called County Line when I still lived in Wellsville [Kansas], I played a show in Greeley, Kansas. The total number of people who showed up was zero. Nobody. It was at a venue with a restaurant on one side and a dance hall on the other. No one showed up, so we talked the owner into opening the door and letting people come in for free. It ended up being amazing. People stayed all night and drank a lot. What they sold in beer alone ended up paying for what we cost. But the first couple of sets were pretty miserable. So that was a bad beginning and a good end. But I've got this optimistic thing in me where I try to block out the bad."

—CHELY WRIGHT

WYNTON MARSALIS

Wynton Marsalis is the most acclaimed trumpet player in the world. Not only has the musician earned nine Grammys spanning jazz to classical, he is one of the few to ever earn a Pulitzer Prize for Music (for "Blood on the Fields," his oratorio about slavery). The New Orleans native (and son of jazz pianist Ellis Marsalis) released his first album in 1981. Since then he's recorded dozens of projects and collaborated with icons from Eric Clapton to Kathleen Battle and Willie Nelson.

"I try to forget them. I don't really know. I've got some I could nominate for it though. We did a Louis Armstrong show once at Jazz at Lincoln Center. It was the Hot Five and Hot Seven. That was a rough one. Nothing about it sounded good. It was painful. Painful. Nothing blew up or anything—just our egos. Sometimes that type of [explosion] is the most painful of all…But you get past the bad gigs quickly. I always wanted to be a musician. And sometimes not everything goes where you think it should. My father told me, 'Do it because you love to do it. Don't put a lot of ulterior motives on it.'"

—*WYNTON MARSALIS*

THE LOST BROTHERS

Irish musicians Mark McCausland and Oisin Leech first bumped into each other at a library in Liverpool, England. Jamming while between stints in other bands, they recorded three acclaimed albums as the acoustic duo The Lost Brothers and managed to get all of them released stateside in 2012. Extensive tours with Glen Hansard of Once fame have brought the pair a wider audience eager to bask in their lush poetry and stark arrangements.

"We remember a gig in Liverpool at a place called the Zanzibar Club in 2010. This turned out to be the worst gig but also the best gig. It was the worst because the promoter—a good friend of ours—went to a lot of trouble to put up posters but nobody came. He lost a lot of money. Nobody was there, and we both had the flu, so we were sweating onstage. There were these blue neon lights; we looked like candles melting.

"On the other hand, our favorite band came—a Liverpool band called The Coral. They were the only people in the audience. We couldn't believe it. We were such huge fans of their music. We were nervous and heartbroken because nobody else showed, but yet our heroes were watching us. The good side of it is they came up after the show and said they enjoyed it. We've since become friends with them.

"But every gig is a gift. We never take any of them for granted. You do have to cherish the good ones."

—*OISIN LEECH,* THE LOST BROTHERS

DRIVIN' 'N' CRYIN'

CREDIT: CARLTON FREEMAN

Atlanta retro-rock act Drivin' 'N' Cryin' built a fervid regional fan base thanks to a potent live reputation. During the alt-rock boom, the ensemble expanded to a national audience through its Southern-tinged single "Fly Me Courageous." The quartet is still going strong, with original members Kevin Kinney (guitar and vocals) and Tim Nielsen (bass) anchoring the lineup.

◆ ◆ ◆

"We played this club in Macon, Georgia, called the Hummingbird. It's this dive downtown on Cherry Street. It's always a great party. Always packed.

"We were staying at the La Quinta on I-75. It's a couple exits toward Atlanta. We parked our trailer and went to bed that night. Luckily, our guitar tech drove back to Atlanta after the show and brought Kevin's guitars in his car—his famous red Mosrite guitar for one.

"I woke up and left with my buddy in his car. But we got a call from our soundman thirty minutes down the road, and he's like, 'Where's the trailer?'

"We're like, 'What are you talking about?'

"Somebody had cut the chain and lifted the loaded, full trailer off our van and stole it. The trailer was gone. Mac [Carter], our former guitar player, immediately put it on Facebook that we'd been robbed, and within a couple minutes we got a call from a pawn shop in Atlanta and found two of his amplifiers.

"We wound up getting the trailer back thirty days

later. It had a couple items in there. There was a bunch of smashed-up stuff. Some drums without cases. Some pedals. They were broken—looked like they'd been sitting out in the rain. The cops found it. The [thieves] dumped it in a parking lot.

"I lost a really sentimental bass that had been on the road with me for years. I lost a mandolin. But you think of the other stuff that we lost, like all the T-shirts and CDs. What are they going to do with those? Will we see a bunch of bums walking around in Drivin' 'N' Cryin' shirts?

"We had a gig a couple days after the trailer was stolen, and we ended up borrowing the opening band's gear. The musical community really reached out to us. Drive-By Truckers lent us amps and guitars. We had insurance, which helped out a little bit. There's this thing through the Grammys called Music Cares. They helped us out. Fans were reaching out. One fan let me borrow his mandolin for a couple months. People were touched by our misfortune and really helped us out. So the experience was bittersweet."

—*TIM NIELSEN,* DRIVIN' 'N' CRYIN'

LED ZEPPELIN

The biggest hard-rock band of all time? Sure. The best? Probably. British icons Robert Plant, Jimmy Page, John Paul Jones and the departed John "Bonzo" Bonham did not in fact go down "like a lead balloon" as The Who's Keith Moon famously predicted. Instead the act sold several hundred million records and ultimately defined the 1970s, in terms of both diverse musical output and legendary excesses.

"The worst show in any band? I can't remember it specifically, but it invariably had something to do with the amount of people onstage getting close to the amount of people in the audience. That is also worst when you're standing there. I don't think it was Zeppelin, but I was with some band and I remember standing onstage in the theater counting the audience—'Three. Four. Five.' That is just soul destroying. But then you can treat it as a paid rehearsal, so maybe it's not so bad after all."

–JOHN PAUL JONES

Few rock stars have ever courted controversy like Ted Nugent—and he likes it that way. The Motor City Madman began as the living embodiment of extreme showmanship during the stadium-rock era, playing thousands of concerts behind hits such as "Cat Scratch Fever" and "Stranglehold." A lifelong commitment to substance abuse–free hedonism coupled with his pro-right-wing stances have ensured that he's lingered as a popular, quotable figure. Whether releasing more than thirty albums, hosting reality TV programs, or publishing books on bow hunting, the talented guitarist and songwriter shows no signs of slowing down. He shared this succinct story about why "it's all good."

INDESCRIBABLY NOT OF THIS EARTH

By Ted Nugent

CREDIT: JENNY RISHER

The beauty of my career, and life, is that I figured out a long, long time ago to eliminate mediocrity and lameness in everything I do. Most important, the elimination of people unwilling to put their heart and soul into being the absolute best that they can be. Hence, by the time I was in my early twenties, I learned to surround myself with American dreamers of excellence and superior dedication, thereby reducing and even eliminating failure and negligence from the equation. Know that my worst concert has been nothing short of brilliant and astonishing. Our best concerts are indescribably not of this earth. We refuse to accept failure and stupid mistakes. Ever. We throttle on, the way it's supposed to be. We kick major ass, so we never get our asses kicked. It is a beautiful thing.

AFTERWORD

THE AUTHOR'S OWN WORST GIG: BLOODY WICHITA

JON NICCUM

During the heyday of alternative rock in the 1990s, I took a quick road trip with my Kansas City–based band Easterday. We were booked at a new club called the Aviator in Wichita, Kansas. The name of the venue was derived from being decorated like an airplane hangar—not surprising in a town nicknamed the "Air Capital of the World."

Despite the whopping size of the fledgling club, we counted a grand total of eighteen people when we took the stage. But a booking was a booking, and we still needed to play whether anyone was paying attention or not.

About midway through the first set, my fretless bass stopped working. I used active electronics in my bass pickups, which meant they were powered by a battery that activated once a cable was plugged into the input jack. It needed a battery replacement about as often as an industrial smoke detector—which was not very often, and quite rare that it would happen during a performance.

Rather than stop the show, and thus prolong the lame gig, I suggested we play a song called "Autumn" that featured a two-minute guitar and voice intro. Because I had spent years teaching guitar and bass lessons, I had perfected routine maintenance on student instruments in blindingly swift fashion. If I could change a string in less than two minutes, I figured I could swap out a battery in about the same stretch.

I plopped down on the corner floor of the stage to execute the procedure. Even though I felt something sharp when I landed, the clock was running so I pressed on. The battery was changed with seconds to spare, and I took my spot at stage right, alongside singer-guitarists Scott and Elaine. About a minute later, I noticed Elaine staring at my butt. This was not a common occurrence.

She pulled back from the microphone and began pointing at the back of my jeans. They were soaked in blood. Apparently, I sat on a broken beer bottle that littered the dark stage—and it had punctured an artery.

"We'll take a quick break," Scott announced over the microphone.

I was ushered into the men's bathroom and started stuffing handfuls of paper towels into my pants to halt the flow. At this point I began to notice my rear was really throbbing. The bleeding continued even as I kept replacing soiled wads of paper towels. A mirror offered a mesmerizing view of the amount of red decorating my blue jeans.

I can't remember much more about the show, other than we muscled through the grueling gig and loaded out. We had driven two different vehicles to Wichita, and on the four-hour ride back to KC (an overnight hotel stay was deemed too expensive), I sat in the front passenger seat of Scott's car.

When Scott eventually dropped me by home, we noticed that my blood had soaked all the way through the towels positioned for me to sit upon. Maybe the incessant bleeding had made me loopy, but I could've sworn the permanent stains on his car seat spread out into the pattern of airplane wings.

ACKNOWLEDGMENTS

Assembly of *The Worst Gig* has now stretched over three decades, and it could not have been accomplished without the encouragement and support of many folks:

Matt Bechtold, my website partner, who took a time-consuming leap of faith with this project.

Monika Verma and the good people at Levine Greenberg Literary Agency.

Jenna Skwarek, Shana Drehs, Deirdre Burgess and everyone at Sourcebooks.

Wendy Molyneux, Jeff Drake, Bjorn Skaptason, Steve Revare, Geoff Harkness, Liz Alderman, Sarah Dickman, Chris Santella, Grant Fitch, Karl Gehring, Laura Kirk, Jai Nitz and Alex Grecian, for lending me their professional advice.

Peter Frampton, for giving me my first Worst Gig story.

My awesome, creative mom, Janet Niccum Miller.

And, finally, Ann and Lola for all their love and energy.

ABOUT THE AUTHOR

Jon Niccum began working as an entertainment journalist in 1993. He is a writer and critic for the *Kansas City Star*. He is the former entertainment editor at the *Lawrence Journal-World* daily newspaper and music and film editor at *The Pitch*, Kansas City's leading alternative weekly.

He's been a contributor to Esquire.com, *Details*, *Village Voice*, *Rotten Tomatoes*, *Miami Herald*, *Phoenix New Times* and *CMJ New Music Monthly*.

CREDIT: GRANT FITCH

Niccum has won several dozen national awards for his writing, including multiple honors from the Suburban Newspapers of America, American Association of Sunday and Feature Editors and National Federation of Press Women, and he was a finalist for a National Music Journalism Award.

Additionally, he has penned the official record-label bios for dozens of artists, including Evanescence, Jeff Beck, Leon Redbone and Joe Satriani.

Prior to a career in journalism, he was a professional guitarist and bassist, performing in bands such as The Budinskis, Easterday and Groovehead. He continues to record with his ongoing cult band Bobby and the Chuxx.

He lives in Lawrence, Kansas.